WORLD OF KNOWLEDGE

The Animal World

Cathy Kilpatrick

Macdonald/Silver Burdett

Editorial Manager	Chester Fisher
Senior Editor	Lynne Sabel
Editor	John Rowlstone
Assistant Editor	Bridget Daly
Series Designers	QED (Alaistair Campbell and Edward Kinsey)
Designer	Mike Blore
Series Consultant	Keith Lye
Consultant	John Stidworthy
Production	Penny Kitchenham
Picture Research	Jenny Golden

© Macdonald Educational Ltd. 1978
First published 1978
Reprinted 1979
Macdonald Educational Ltd.
Holywell House
Worship Street
London EC2A 2EN

Published in the
United States by
Silver Burdett Company
Morristown, N.J.
1980 Printing
ISBN 0-382-06403-8

World of Knowledge

This book breaks new ground in the method it uses to present information to the reader. The unique page design combines narrative with an alphabetical reference section and it uses colourful photographs, diagrams and illustrations to provide an instant and detailed understanding of the book's theme. The main body of information is presented in a series of chapters that cover, in depth, the subject of this book. At the bottom of each page is a reference section which gives, in alphabetical order, concise articles which define, or enlarge on, the topics discussed in the chapter. Throughout the book, the use of SMALL CAPITALS in the text directs the reader to further information that is printed in the reference section. The same method is used to cross-reference entries within each reference section. Finally, there is a comprehensive index at the end of the book that will help the reader find information in the text, illustrations and reference sections. The quality of the text, and the originality of its presentation, ensure that this book can be read both for enjoyment and for the most up-to-date information on the subject.

Contents

Animals Great and Small — 3
The land, sea and air are filled with a tremendous variety of living animals. All these animals, which differ greatly in size and shape, are specially adapted so that they can survive and breed successfully.

Mammals — 9
Compared with birds or fishes, there are only a few species of mammals. But, since the extinction of the dinosaurs over 60 million years ago, mammals have dominated the land. Other mammals also live in the sea and some are even airborne.

Birds — 17
The ancestors of birds were toothed reptiles, but their modern descendants are fully adapted to life in the air, with light bones and streamlined bodies. The annual migrations of some birds are still not fully understood by man.

Reptiles and Amphibians — 26
The first land vertebrates were amphibians, part of their lives being spent in water. Their descendants, the reptiles, were the first true land animals because they did not return to the water to breed.

Fishes — 33
Fishes were the first animals with backbones. Most fishes live in Sun-warmed surface waters, but some have adapted to life in icy polar waters and others exist in ocean trenches some 11 kilometres deep.

Arthropods — 39
Arthropods are the most numerous of all animals. They include insects (the largest animal class of all), crustaceans, arachnids, centipedes and millipedes. The number of recorded insects is increasing as new species are discovered.

Other Invertebrates — 45
The invertebrate world includes many other species besides the arthropods. They range from the simplest animals – microscopic protozoans, which some botanists claim as plants – to the giant squid and the Portuguese man o' war.

Adaptation to Environment — 49
Ecology is the study of animals and plants in their natural habitats. By studying an animal as part of an animal and plant community, we can better understand the inter-relationships which hold together the delicate balance of nature.

Man and Animals — 57
Throughout history, many species have become extinct as better adapted species replaced them. But man has created a crisis in the natural world. Today, we are just beginning to understand the dangers of upsetting the balance of nature.

Index — 65

Introduction

The Animal World is a broad survey of the animal kingdom and animal behaviour in all its fascinating variety, both on land, in the sea and in the air. There are more than 1,000,000 species of animals, not including the enormous number of extinct species which we know about only from their fossil remains. Living species range from the blue whale, which is probably the largest and heaviest animal that has ever lived on Earth, to minute protozoans which can be seen only through a microscope. **The Animal World** also shows how each species has a special relationship with other animals and plants around it and how each species has evolved particular adaptations to its environment which enable it to live and breed successfully. However, should this environment be destroyed or altered, especially by the activities of man, entire species can be threatened with extinction.

The land, sea and air are filled with a tremendous variety of living animals. All these animals, which differ greatly in size and shape, are specially adapted so that they can survive and breed successfully.

Animals Great and Small

There are more than one million different kinds, or species, of living animals on the planet Earth, ranging in almost infinite variety from domestic dogs and cats to wild tigers and elephants and birds, fish, beetles and butterflies. New species are being discovered all the time by scientists and naturalists. This enormous variety of animal life has evolved many different ways of moving about from place to place, such as walking, crawling, swimming, hopping, flying, gliding and burrowing.

An animal usually adapts to living in a particular habitat in its ENVIRONMENT. Living creatures can usually be found in almost every part of the Earth. For example, polar bears combat the same inhospitable climate of the north polar regions as do penguins at the South Pole. In the marine environment, certain fishes are equipped for life at the bottom of the ocean and are able to withstand the terrific pressure of the waters there. Some animals are adapted to live on or inside the bodies of animals and are known as PARASITES, while others actually form a mutually beneficial association known as symbiosis.

Man is the most intelligent species in the ANIMAL KINGDOM. He has certainly adapted himself to live in almost all the environments found on Earth and dominates life today. However, when we study the various numbers of species in the main groups, we discover, amazingly, that the greatest variety of species is not in man's group, the mammals, but in the Arthropoda, a group of the INVERTEBRATES. The Arthropoda includes beetles, crabs, butterflies, wasps and flies. Over 900,000 species are identified in this group, all of them having hard, horny skeletons on the outside of their bodies. Fishes, birds, amphibians, reptiles and mammals, all of which are VERTEBRATES (also known as CHORDATES), account for only 45,000 species. Perhaps more

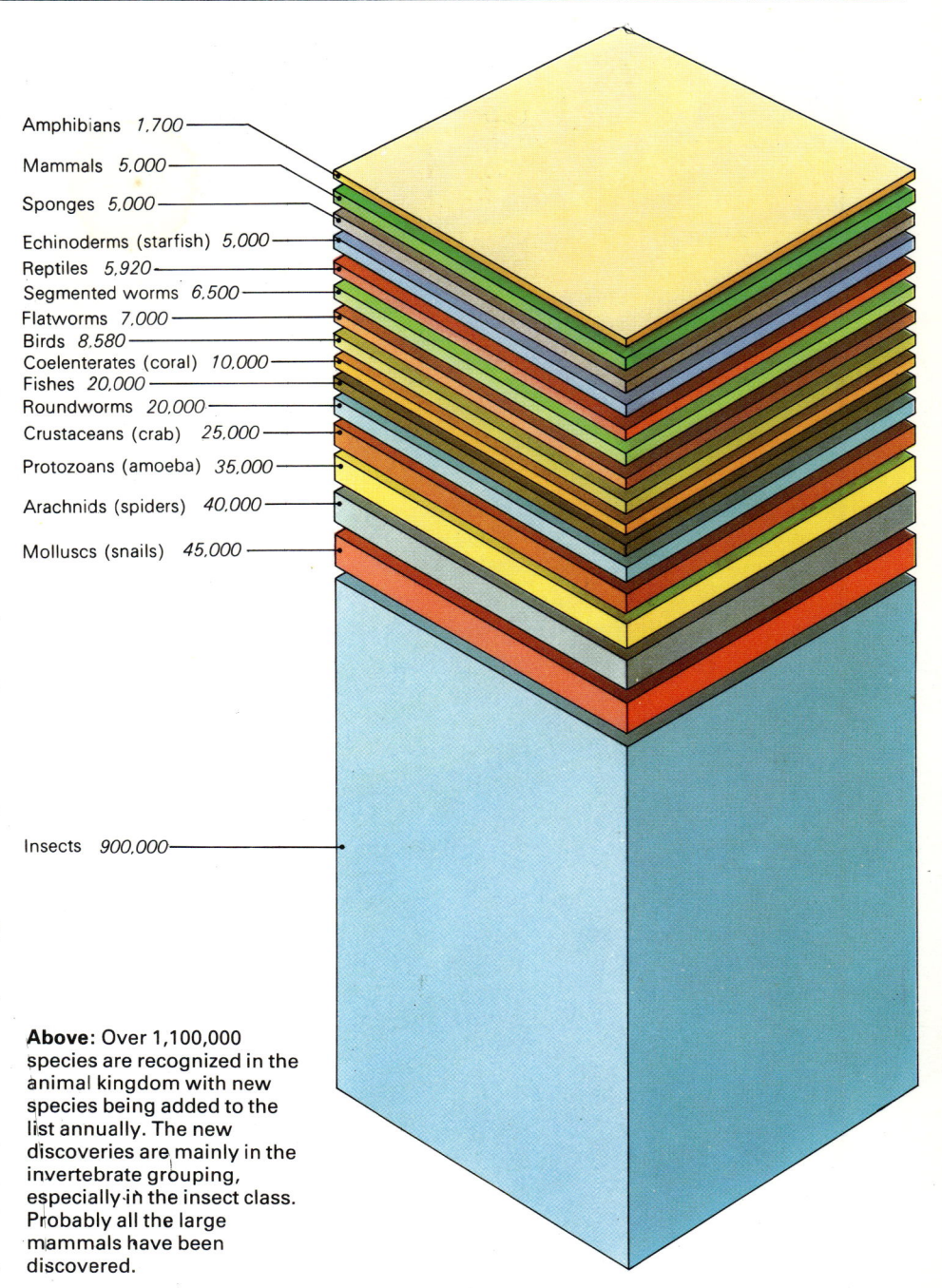

Amphibians 1,700
Mammals 5,000
Sponges 5,000
Echinoderms (starfish) 5,000
Reptiles 5,920
Segmented worms 6,500
Flatworms 7,000
Birds 8,580
Coelenterates (coral) 10,000
Fishes 20,000
Roundworms 20,000
Crustaceans (crab) 25,000
Protozoans (amoeba) 35,000
Arachnids (spiders) 40,000
Molluscs (snails) 45,000
Insects 900,000

Above: Over 1,100,000 species are recognized in the animal kingdom with new species being added to the list annually. The new discoveries are mainly in the invertebrate grouping, especially in the insect class. Probably all the large mammals have been discovered.

Reference

A Animal kingdom includes all the known species of animals in the world. The kingdom is split up into various divisions in a system of CLASSIFICATION.
Aristotle (384-322 BC) was one of the early Greek thinkers. In his philosophical works on biology he showed the importance of change in nature. He understood that the speck of matter in a hen's egg becomes, by definite stages, a chicken.

C Cambrian period (570-500 million years ago). Many FOSSILS are found in these earliest rocks.
Carboniferous period

Wallaby with young in pouch

(345-280 million years ago). The climate in many parts of the world was then warm and moist. Dense, swampy forests were found on land.
Chordata are all the animals that possess a notochord (the forerunner to the backbone). Among the first chordates were the graptolites, an extinct group of marine animals which thrived in the CAMBRIAN PERIOD.
Classification is the system in biology by which organisms are arranged into a series of groups within groups according to certain anatomical characteristics. The smallest unit is a species. This includes individuals that are biologically the same and will interbreed

naturally. Groups of similar species form a genus, with groups of genera forming a family. Families form an order, orders form a class, classes form a phylum, and phyla form a kingdom. The system was devised by Carolus Linnaeus (1707-78), a Swedish biologist.
Cretaceous period (135-65 million years ago). Its name comes from the Latin *creta*, meaning chalk. Many of the DINOSAURS evolved during the Cretaceous period.
Cuvier, Georges (1769-1832), rejected all ideas of changes in animal form and

surprising is that of over one million species of animals, some 95 per cent have no internal skeleton at all, many of them also being invisible to the human eye.

Evolution of life

The modern diversity of animal life is a result of over 500 million years of evolutionary development. For generations, NATURAL SELECTION has favoured the individuals best adapted to their way of life by eliminating their inferior competitors. This theory was first put forward by Charles DARWIN and Alfred WALLACE in the 19th century. Evolution is still at work today. Animal species are continually adapting to their changing surroundings or environment. Peppered moths originally evolved to live on lichen-covered trees as they offered a protective camouflage. The moth's wings have since darkened in colour to match a new environment – that of the polluted towns and countryside.

Early theories about the origin of life now seem rather amusing. Thales (640–546 BC) believed water was the origin of life, while Anaximenes (c. 500 BC) said all things came from the air. Two other strange theories were once believed; that orchids gave birth to birds and small men, and that birds were born from flying fish, lions from sea lions and men from mermen. Early students of theology accepted the theory of creation as told in the book of *Genesis* in the Bible. It was not until the late 17th and 18th centuries that scientists doubted these early theories and advanced new ones. Martin Lister (1638–1712) and Robert Hooke (1635–1703) discovered a great deal by linking the fossils they found with different rock layers. The first startling new theory put forward was probably in 1788, when James Hutton (1726–97) published *Theory of the Earth* explaining the past history of the earth through 'UNIFORMITARIANISM'. Carolus Linnaeus (1707–78), the Swedish biologist, grouped the species into a convenient CLASSIFICATION system, while Jean LAMARCK (1744–1829) was the first person to tackle how species originated.

Today we have an excellent idea of how evolution has taken place with many kinds of evidence helping to build up a picture of the past. It seems to have begun in the sea and progressed onto the land in a series of phases when certain animal groups, for example the amphibians, became dominant for a time. The amphibians were later eclipsed by the more adaptable reptiles. The history of present-day species has been built up through PALAEONTOLOGY (the study of fossils). Some living forms, such as the king crab and scorpion, are almost identical to their relatives that lived millions of years ago. Perhaps the most celebrated of these LIVING FOSSILS is the coelacanth. This lobe-finned fish was thought to be completely extinct until a specimen was caught in 1938.

Over half the animals that have ever lived are already EXTINCT. Fossil evidence is all that remains of them. The DINOSAURS, PTEROSAURS and mammoths (hairy elephants with long tusks) proved unable to adapt quickly enough to the changing conditions and so died out.

The Australian marsupials have undergone their own private evolution. In most continents the placental mammals proved to be too much competition for the marsupials, but in the relative isolation of Australia they have evolved to fill the ecological roles taken up elsewhere by non-marsupial species. This process is known as adaptive radiation.

Above: The Tuatara lives in New Zealand. It is something of a living fossil, for creatures very similar to it existed about 200 million years ago in the Triassic period.

Above: Ammonites are a wholly extinct class of molluscs known from the early Devonian to late Cretaceous times. A diverse group, some species measured over a metre in diameter.

---

stated that life had been repeatedly wiped out and replaced by new species. This theory was known as catastrophism.

Darwin, Charles (1809-82), was the man who put forward in the 1850s the theory of NATURAL SELECTION and the survival of the fittest to explain how animals have come to change and evolve through the ages. He accompanied the HMS *Beagle* on a voyage to South America and Australasia in 1831 as an unpaid naturalist. When Darwin read the essay *The principles of population* by Thomas Malthus, he realized that under the very competitive conditions in the animal and plant world, any variations of species which continued would have to be those which increased the organism's ability to leave fertile offspring. The variations which decreased the animals' or plants' numbers would eventually be eliminated and thus 'natural selection' took place. Darwin revealed his thoughts, and those of WALLACE, in a paper to the Linnaean Society in July 1858. In the following year he published *The Origin of Species*.

Devonian period (395-345 million years ago). Fishes were dominant in the seas, and it was from the species with lungs and limb-like paired fins that amphibians evolved late in this period.

Dinosaurs were the largest land animals that have lived on the Earth. No man has seen any of these prehistoric monsters alive as they died out 65 million years ago. FOSSILS tell us what they looked like. There were 2 main orders, *Saurischia* and *Ornithischia*. Many dinosaurs walked on their hind legs and had massive tails in order to maintain their balance when moving. The crocodile family is the surviving group most closely related to dinosaurs.

Embryology covers an animal's progress from the fertilization of an ovum (or egg) up until birth or hatching.

Environment is the term used to describe the conditions in which an organism lives. These include temperature, light and water, as well as other organisms.

1870s cartoon of Darwin

Animals Great and Small

Pre-Cambrian	Cambrian	Ordovician	Silurian	Devonian	Carboniferous	Permian	Triassic	Jurassic	Cretaceous	Tertiary	Quaternary
600	500		400		300		200		100		0

Invertebrates: Trilobite, Scorpion, King crab, Bird-eating spider

Fishes: Cephalaspis, Dinichthys, Australian lungfish, Shark, African perch

Amphibians: Ichthyostega, Eryops, Frog

Reptiles: Dimetrodon, Stegosaurus, Nile crocodile

Birds: Archaeopteryx, Great tit

Mammals: Hyracotherium, Gorilla

Key
- Age of Invertebrates
- Age of Fishes
- Age of Amphibians
- Age of Reptiles
- Age of Mammals

Above: Life originated in the oceans of the Pre-Cambrian period when conditions enabled single-celled creatures to form from non-living matter. These evolved slowly into the numerous soft-bodied animals called the invertebrates. The first animals with backbones evolved some 500 million years ago. Of the 5 classes of vertebrates, the bird class was the last to evolve.

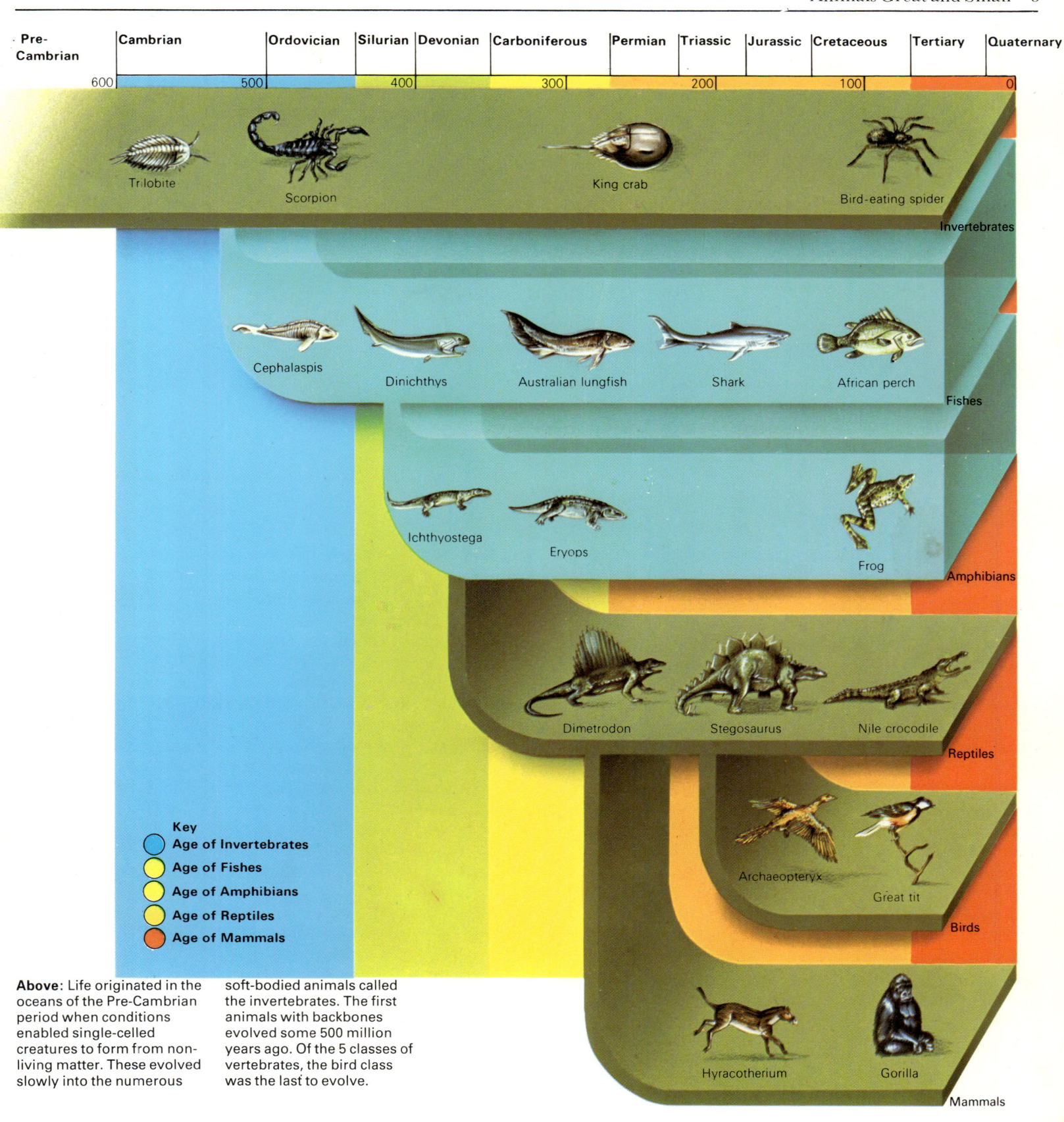

Evolution means 'unfolding' and describes the gradual process by which all the life forms today have evolved from earlier forms which lived on the Earth millions of years ago. Our present views are based on the theories of Charles DARWIN and Gregor MENDEL.

Tyrannosaurus Rex

Extinction is the term used when an animal or plant dies out. This is the result when the population of a certain species loses more members than it gains through reproduction. This might be brought about by natural changes in the animal's environment, such as climatic changes, that it cannot adapt to. More recently the changes have been caused by man's activities and interference.

F Fossils are the hardened remains of plants or animals, or impressions of their forms, preserved in rocks. Generally, only the hard parts like skeletons are preserved. They may be partly or wholly replaced by minerals deposited from circulating water. Fossils are formed in many ways. A common method is when a dead organism is covered by mud or sand, which later changes into rocks; this process can take millions of years.

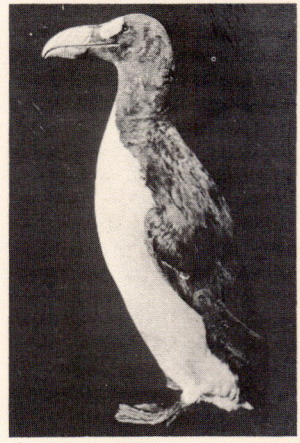

Great Auk (extinct)

H Habitat is a place or particular ENVIRONMENT, such as a sea shore or a woodland, in which an animal or plant lives.

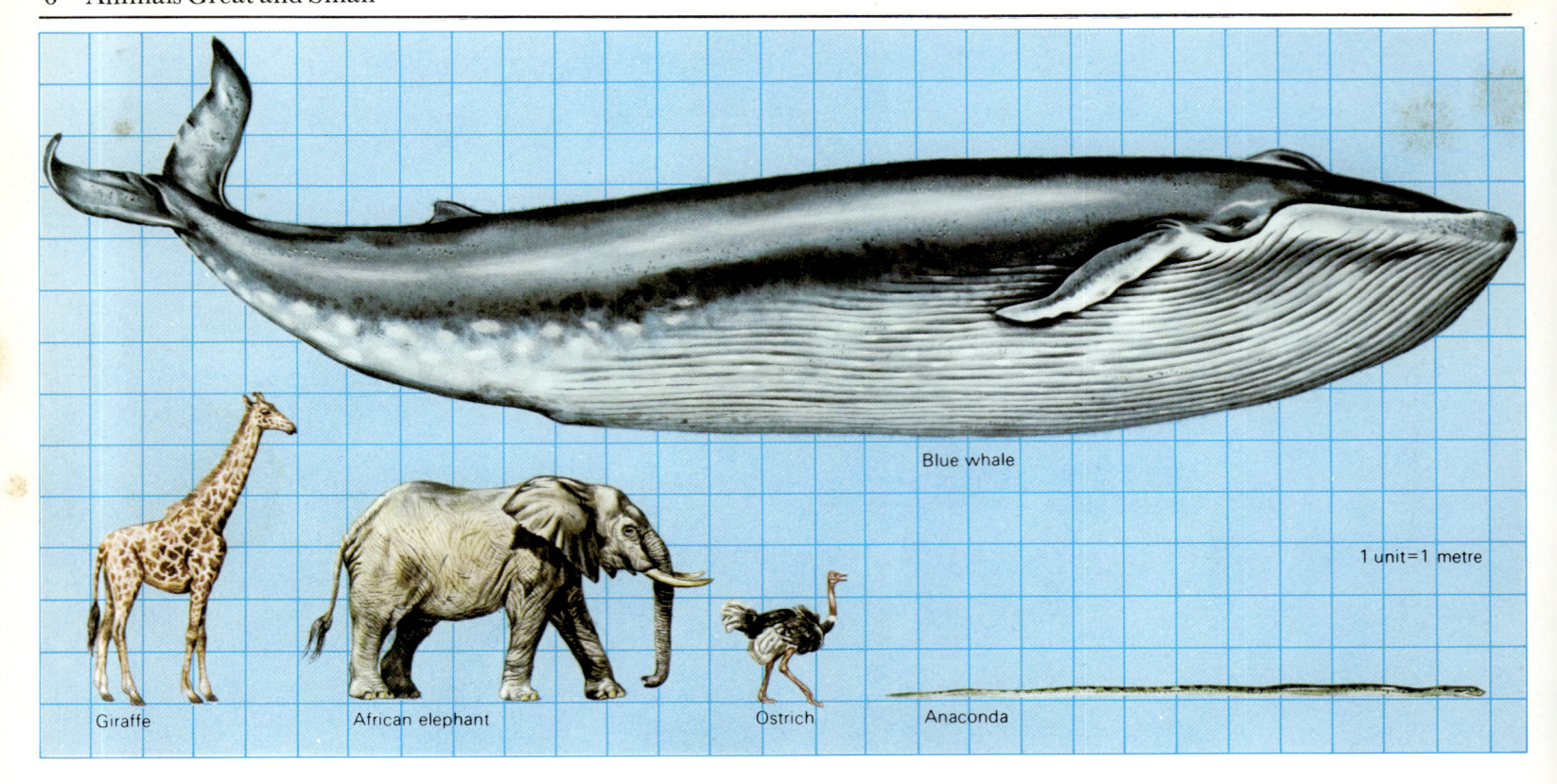

Animals Great and Small

Blue whale
1 unit = 1 metre
Giraffe
African elephant
Ostrich
Anaconda

The record holders

The enormous variety in the animal kingdom is best shown in the records of the largest and smallest animals in a group. Most whales are quite large but the largest and heaviest marine mammal is the blue whale. This species is also known as the sulphur-bottom whale because of the yellow film of microscopic plants (diatoms) often found on its underside. A blue whale is at its heaviest after the summer when it has fed itself on krill (tiny shrimp-like animals) and put on lots of blubber for the winter months when food is scarce. An African elephant put next to a blue whale looks quite dwarfed. In fact, about ten African elephants could stand head to tail on a blue whale's back. However, the African or savanna elephant is the largest land animal alive today and indeed has no enemies apart from man in its grassland home.

The African landscape is also the home of the world's tallest mammal. The giraffe's head towers some five metres above the ground. The greatest recorded height is 5·8 metres, which is 1·4 metres taller than a London double-decker bus!

The largest bird – the ostrich – is also found on the grasslands of Africa. This flightless bird, or ratite, stands about 2·5 metres tall and on average weighs 120 to 127 kilograms. The heaviest bird that can still fly is the kori bustard of East and South Africa where adult cock birds average about 12 kilograms, although there is a record of one tipping the scales at 18 kilograms.

At the other end of the bird world, the smallest in size and weight are the tiny hummingbirds, nature's helicopters from tropical America. The smallest is actually found only on the island of Cuba. This is the bee hummingbird, the male of which has a body length of 58 millimetres and weighs about 20 grams, which is less than a sphinx moth.

The giants of the reptile world are the notorious man-eating crocodiles and the constrictor snakes. The largest reptile is the estuarine crocodile which ranges from India eastwards through the Malay archipelago to northern Australia. Adult males average 3·6 to 4·3 metres in length and weigh about 450 kilograms, but even older ones can be half as heavy again. The largest on record is 8·2 metres

Above: Some of the record breakers of the animal kingdom are shown here. The blue whale is the largest and heaviest animal in the world; a female measured 33·5 metres in length. On land the tallest is the African giraffe, while the African elephant is the heaviest, up to 10·7 tonnes. The ostrich is the largest bird although it cannot fly, and the largest snake is the anaconda.

Above: The smallest bird is the bee hummingbird, here compared with a bumble bee for size. Adult specimens measure 90 mm long and weigh between 3·5–4·5 grams.

Invertebrates are all those animals that do not possess a backbone. This includes organisms such as amoeba, sponges, starfish, worms, insects, snails, jellyfish and sea squirts. The animals with backbones are called VERTEBRATES.

Jurassic period (195–135 million years ago) saw the rise of the largest dinosaurs.

Lamarck, Jean Baptiste (1744–1829), was a French biologist who first put forward a theory of the inheritance of acquired characters to account for EVOLUTION. He believed that changes in an animal's conditions created new needs for it. These new needs lead to new methods of behaviour and involved fresh uses, or non-usage, of existing organs of the body. Lamarck gave the rather poor example of the giraffe to illustrate his point. Lamarck inferred that this animal in trying to feed on foliage that grows high above the ground, stretches its neck and legs in the process. As a result, many generations later the giraffe had developed into an animal with very long legs and neck.

Jean Baptiste Lamarck

Living fossil is the term given to many modern animals and plants that are recognizable as relatives of prehistoric forms, and have not greatly changed their form for millions of years. The coelacanth is a living fossil in the fish world. This lobe-finned fish was thought

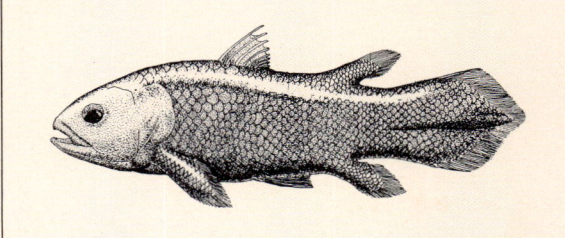

Coelacanth

for a killer crocodile from the Philippines.

There are many exaggerated claims about the longest and heaviest of snakes – the anaconda of tropical South America. Although these serpents are claimed to have been seen over 12 metres long, most adults never grow to more than six metres. However, a snake shot in the Upper Orinoco River, eastern Colombia, in 1944 was measured at 11·3 metres.

Arthropods are limited in size by the fact that their hard external skeleton has to be shed, or moulted, each time they want to increase in size. The heaviest insect is the Goliath beetle, but it only weighs up to 95 grams. Some crabs may weigh up to 18 kilograms.

Certain animals in the animal kingdom still hold records although they are not the largest, heaviest, or smallest. These are the ones that are able to live in extreme habitats, such as at a very high altitude or great depth.

Speed

The popular tale of the hare and the tortoise clearly shows the relative speeds of the two animals. Although the hare moved fast, almost 400 times faster than the slow, plodding tortoise, it lost that particular race through taking a nap in the middle. Animals have evolved different methods of movement and differing speeds to suit their particular needs and environment. In the air, wings have proved to be the perfect equipment. In water, the animal is usually streamlined in shape (like a torpedo), as this design is best suited to dealing with the water's

Below: A chart showing the altitudes and depths that certain members of the animal kingdom can live at. These are compared with the deepest mine shaft, ocean trench and highest mountain.

3 Tortoiseshell butterfly

4 Common toad

1 Alpine chough
2 Yak
5 Seal
6 Sperm whale
7 Brotulid
8 Red shrimp

---

to be extinct for over 65 million years until in 1938, one specimen was caught off South Africa.

M **Mendel,** Gregor (1822–84), was an Austrian priest who discovered a mechanism of inheritance (the transmission of characters from parents to offspring). He performed thousands of experiments with the garden pea to show genetic inheritance.
Mesozoic era is from the TRIASSIC to the end of the CRETACEOUS, and is often called the Age of Reptiles.

N **Natural selection** is the main process by which animal and plant species undergo evolutionary change. Within any given species, there are always variations in the characteristics of individuals. Some of these individuals will have certain characteristics that give them a better chance of survival in a changing environment.

O **Ordovician period** (500–440 million years ago). The first fossil remains of vertebrates have been found in rocks of this period.

P **Palaeontology** is the study of FOSSILS of animals and plants in order to understand what life was like in the Earth's past.
Parasites are organisms living in or on another organism which acts as the host. They obtain food from the host and are usually harmful to it. A tapeworm, for example, lives inside the gut of an animal, and is an internal parasite. A blood-sucking tick attaches itself with powerful jaws to a mammal's body and is therefore an external parasite.
Pre-Cambrian period is the general name given to the first 4,000 million years of the Earth's history.
Pterosaurs are animals be-

Gregor Mendel

Pterosaur

longing to an extinct order of flying reptiles. Their 'wings' consisted of webs of skin stretched between the hind legs and body and the ex-

Animals Great and Small

Far left: Flying fish, here seen in the Red Sea, have large pectoral fins that can be spread like wings. Flights can last for over 30 seconds and the distance travelled can be up to 350 metres.
Left: Ostriches live on the African savanna grasslands. Although they are the largest living birds, they are unable to fly.

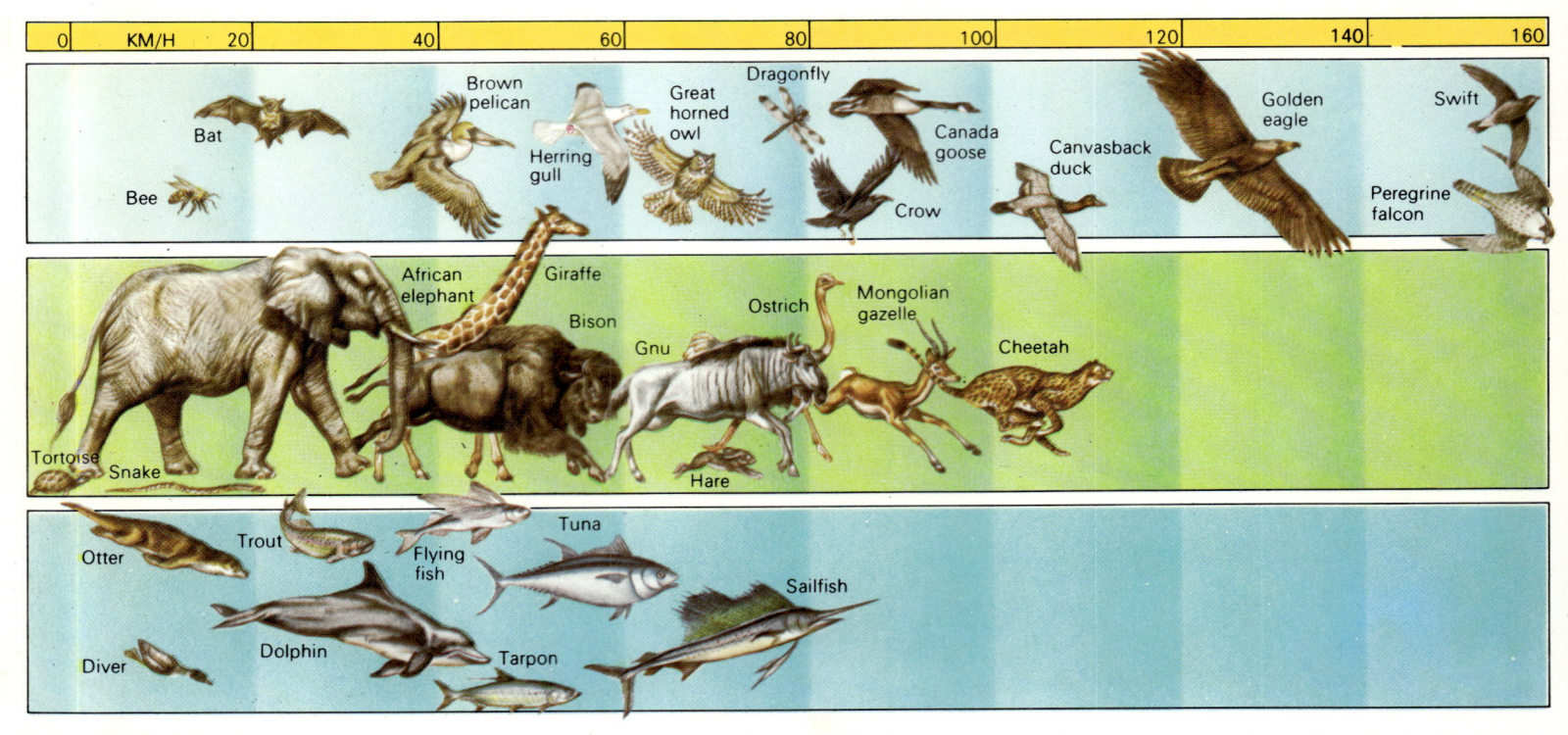

Above: The fastest animals on land, sea and air are here compared. Air offers the least resistance, so the fastest speeds are attained. Streamlining is important in all categories. On land, mammals are the fastest movers, and although some mammalian species, such as dolphins and otters, are fast movers in water, the fishes are the fastest swimmers. Because of the greater resistance offered by water, the speeds reached are much slower than those achieved by animals on land or in the air.

drag effect. Land animals are equipped with legs which can vary in number from just two to over 100 pairs. Certain creatures, such as snakes, are legless, however, and they too have developed their own method of movement.

If all the animals of the world were pitted against one another in a race, the birds would outclass all the others. The swifts are well named as they are among the fastest of birds. A spine-tail swift is claimed to hold the record at 352 kilometres per hour, although this is rather doubtful. This swift has certainly exceeded 161 kilometres per hour so it would still be the fastest.

On land, four legs are generally more useful than two. The cheetah is the fastest animal over a short distance at about 90 kilometres per hour. However, a Mongolian gazelle and an American pronghorn antelope could keep up a speed of over 80 kilometres per hour for much further. A gazelle, which is being hunted by a cheetah, will often escape if it can jump and turn in the first few hundred metres. The cheetah is not so expert at quick manoeuvres, and after about 350 metres the cheetah will involuntarily pull up absolutely exhausted. The same story is also true of a hare being hunted by a fox, or a mouse attempting to evade a pursuing weasel. In water, quick movement is more difficult because the medium is about 800 times denser than air. The fastest swimmer is probably the sailfish, which can move at over 80 kilometres per hour.

Although speed and movement are important animal features, there are some creatures that do not move at all. The corals, barnacles and some shellfish become fixed to a solid object, such as a rock, early in life and remain there until they die.

---

tended 4th digit in the forelimb.

Q **Quaternary period** (the last 2 million years). It contains the Pleistocene and the Holocene (or Recent) epochs.

S **Silurian period** (440–395 million years ago). It was during this period that the first land organisms (plants) evolved.
Species is the smallest unit of CLASSIFICATION commonly used. All the members of a species have similar characteristics and look alike. In most animals and plants, only members of the same species can interbreed to produce fertile offspring.
Streamlining is the adaptation shown by certain animals that enables them to move fast and efficiently through their environment. Dolphins, mackerel and tunny fish, for example, are smooth, torpedo-shaped aquatic animals. This streamlining allows them to speed through the water. Eagles, swifts, swallows and ducks are streamlined to fly fast through the air. Flight is explained on page 18.

T **Tertiary period** (65–2 million years ago). It is often termed the Age of Mammals.
Triassic period (225–195 million years ago). The dominant aquatic animals were the ichthyosaurs, while on land, reptiles had taken over from the large amphibians.

U **Uniformitarianism** was the explanation of the past history of the Earth put forward by James Hutton (1726–97) in his essay entitled *A Theory of the Earth*. The idea being that whatever processes are operating today also operated in the past with similar results. 'The present is the key to the past.'

V **Vertebrates** are those animals grouped in the most important sub-phylum of the Chordata and includes the fish, amphibians, reptiles, birds and mammals. They differ from all other chordates in having a skull, surrounding a well-developed brain, and a skeleton of cartilage or bone. They are often defined as animals with backbones. INVERTEBRATES are animals without backbones.

W **Wallace,** Alfred Russel (1823–1913), was an English naturalist who reached the same evolutionary views as DARWIN but whilst working amongst animals in South America and south-east Asia. He argued that species evolved slowly and the survival of the fittest would lead to new types. Wallace sent his beliefs in an article to Darwin. This, together with a summary of Darwin's work, was published in 1858.

Compared with birds or fishes, there are only a few species of mammals. But, since the extinction of the dinosaurs over 60 million years ago, mammals have dominated the land. Other mammals also live in the sea and some are even air-borne.

Mammals

Although relatively few in numbers compared to other groups of animals, the mammals contain the most successful and also the most conspicuous animal forms on our planet. An important feature of this group is that mammals are the only animals that have hair – sometimes called wool or fur – covering their bodies. However, there are some mammals that are relatively hairless. The ELEPHANT, although quite hairy when it is born, loses most of it as it gets older. The sea-dwelling DOLPHINS and WHALES have also lost their fur during the course of evolution.

Hair is a most important factor in maintaining a mammal's body heat, as it forms an insulating (heat-trapping) layer around the body. Mammals and birds are warm-blooded, that is to say they can make heat inside their bodies. This enables them to digest food faster, move faster and grow faster than cold-blooded animals.

Female mammals can also produce milk in mammary glands. These supply their young with important nourishment during early childhood. Pouched mammals, or MARSUPIALS, although giving birth to embryo-like young, suckle their young in a pouch until they are fully developed. The most primitive mammals are the egg-layers, known as the MONOTREMES.

Although there are only 4,200 species of mammals compared with 8,500 birds, or 20,000 bony fishes, the class is a very successful one. Mammals can be found in the air (BATS); in the tops of trees (squirrels, MONKEYS, LEMURS); browsing on the forest floor (DEER, wild pigs); grazing on the grasslands (horses, ANTELOPES,

Right: There are 19 orders of mammals. A mammal is an animal that feeds its young with milk secreted by the mother's mammary glands. Most mammals are covered with hair, sometimes called wool or fur.

Edentata: Anteater
Pholidota: Pangolin
Rodentia: Beaver
Cetacea: Dolphin
Hyracoidea: Hyrax
Sirenia: Manatee
Perissodactyla: Tapir
Artiodactyla: Hippopotamus
Monotremata: Platypus
Marsupialia: Koala
Insectivora: Mole
Dermoptera: Colugo
Chiroptera: Bat
Primates: Lemur
Carnivora: Bear
Pinnipedia: Seal
Lagomorpha: Hare 
Proboscidea: Elephant 
Tubulidentata: Aardvark 

Reference

A Aardvarks are the single species of the order Tubulidentata. They live in Africa and have pig-like bodies with a thick, tapering tail and a long tongue which sweeps up termites.
Anteater is the name given to those mammals adapted to feeding on termites and other soft-bodied insects. These include PANGOLINS, aardvarks and ECHIDNAS.
Antelopes are graceful runners of the order ARTIODACTY-LA. They are found mainly in Africa and the family includes springbok, impala, gerenuk and gazelles.

Tamandua, or Lesser Anteater

Apes differ from all other PRIMATES in the absence of a tail, greater brain capacity, longer arms and no cheek-pouches. They are man's nearest relatives and include the gibbon, orang-utan, chimpanzee and gorilla.
Armadillos are armour-plated relatives of the SLOTHS and ANTEATERS. They are only found in the Americas and include 9-banded, giant, and fairy armadillos.
Artiodactyla. This even-toed ungulate order includes pigs, camels, deer, antelopes and cattle. They all have 2 or 4 toes on each foot, complex stomachs and the majority have horns or antlers which are placed on the crown.

B Baboons are Old World MONKEYS that have adapted to living and hunting on the ground. They live in groups of up to 200 mem-

Baboon

Mammals

Left: The mole is highly adapted for an underground life with its broad fore-paws that act like highly-efficient shovels, and its tiny eyes. The hind feet kick back the loosened earth.

Right: Many aquatic mammals and birds have webbed feet. This increase in surface area aids movement through the water. Here a European otter shows off his webbed feet.

cattle); high up on mountainsides (GOATS, sheep); living beneath the Earth's surface (MOLES, LEMMINGS); in undergrowth (RODENTS); as active predators (LIONS, BEARS, mongooses) and as aquatic inhabitants (WHALES and SEALS).

Most mammals have evolved a system of movement that uses all four legs on the ground, although there are a few exceptions. Man, for one, has become upright in his stance. His action is known as bi-pedal movement. He only walks or crawls on four legs as a baby. The CHIMPANZEE, GORILLA and ORANG-UTAN are relatives of man and are all grouped in the ape family. They usually move on all fours, but can walk on their hind legs and use their arms to balance as they waddle along. The GIBBON, another of man's relatives, is able to walk on two legs but usually swings from branch to branch using its long arms.

Depending on how fast they need to move, land animals have evolved various different stances. For example, fairly slow-moving animals like BEARS, BABOONS, APES and man, walk on the soles of their feet (plantigrade). In others the sole of the foot is raised, giving greater length to the leg and the animal moves on the digits of the toes and fingers. This method is found in dogs, cats, mongooses, rabbits and rats. The fastest animals have the longest legs in proportion to their body and this is achieved where the mammal moves on tip toes, or the nails or claws of the feet have enlarged and become hooves. The hoofed mammals, or ungulates, all move in this way (unguligrade), either raised up on one or three toes (Perissodactyls) or two or four toes (Artiodactyls).

Tree-dwelling mammals have grasping hands with five fingers. Often one of the fingers is opposed to the other four forming a thumb. This enables the hand to get a firm grasp of a branch. This is seen in most monkeys, apes, and lower PRIMATES such as tarsiers.

Mammals that burrow under the ground have developed digging equipment. Rabbits, AARDVARKS, ARMADILLOS and prairie dogs have strong thick claws. An armadillo, if pursued, can burrow out of harm's way quicker than a man can dig a hole with a spade. The champion digger is the mole whose front feet are like living shovels.

Several mammals have left the land to spend most of their lives in water. To move efficiently through the water both legs and arms have usually become flipper-shaped as in seals and sealions. In whales and dolphins the fore flippers are present and help with steering, but most of the propulsive force comes from the strong muscular tail.

The webbed feet of the BEAVER and otter help push the animals through the water and the beaver has a splendid paddle-like tail which acts like a rudder in water and a prop on land when the beaver is busy chopping down trees with its strong, gnawing front teeth.

Mammals have also taken to the air. There are over 980 species of bat. This order is second only

---

bers. They feed on fruit, insects and small animals.
Bats are the only mammals capable of true flight. There are two groups, the fruit bats and the insectivorous or carnivorous bats. Fruit bats use their sensitive eyes whereas the rest use echolocation to find their way about. The few families that live in colder climates either hibernate or migrate.
Bears are heavily-built, practically tailless carnivores with broad flat feet. Most bears are omnivorous in diet, but the polar bear is a true flesh-eater.

Beavers are amphibious RODENTS of Eurasia and North America. They have a broad, flat tail which acts as a rudder, and live in family units, building a dam across a stream with a lodge of aspen and willow upstream.

Black bear

Beaver

Bison, or North American buffalo, and the European bison, or wisent, were almost exterminated by man, but are now protected. The American bison has the shaggier coat of the two.

Camels are either Bactrian (two-humped) or Arabian (one-humped). Both types have adapted to life in the harsh deserts.
Caribou are North American REINDEER. Both sexes grow antlers. They have adapted to Arctic conditions with thick coats and broad, flat deeply-cleft hoofs.

Carnivora. This order contains a wide variety of mammals including cats, dogs, bears, otters, hyenas, etc. Their jaw-line and tooth structure has adapted for eating flesh, although some will also eat vegetation.
Cat refers to both the various domestic breeds and to wild cats such as the lion, jaguar, leopard and lynx.
Cattle are all ARTIODACTYLS and include both wild species such as the Indian buffalo and YAK and the domestic breeds (shorthorns, jerseys).
Cetacea. This order con-

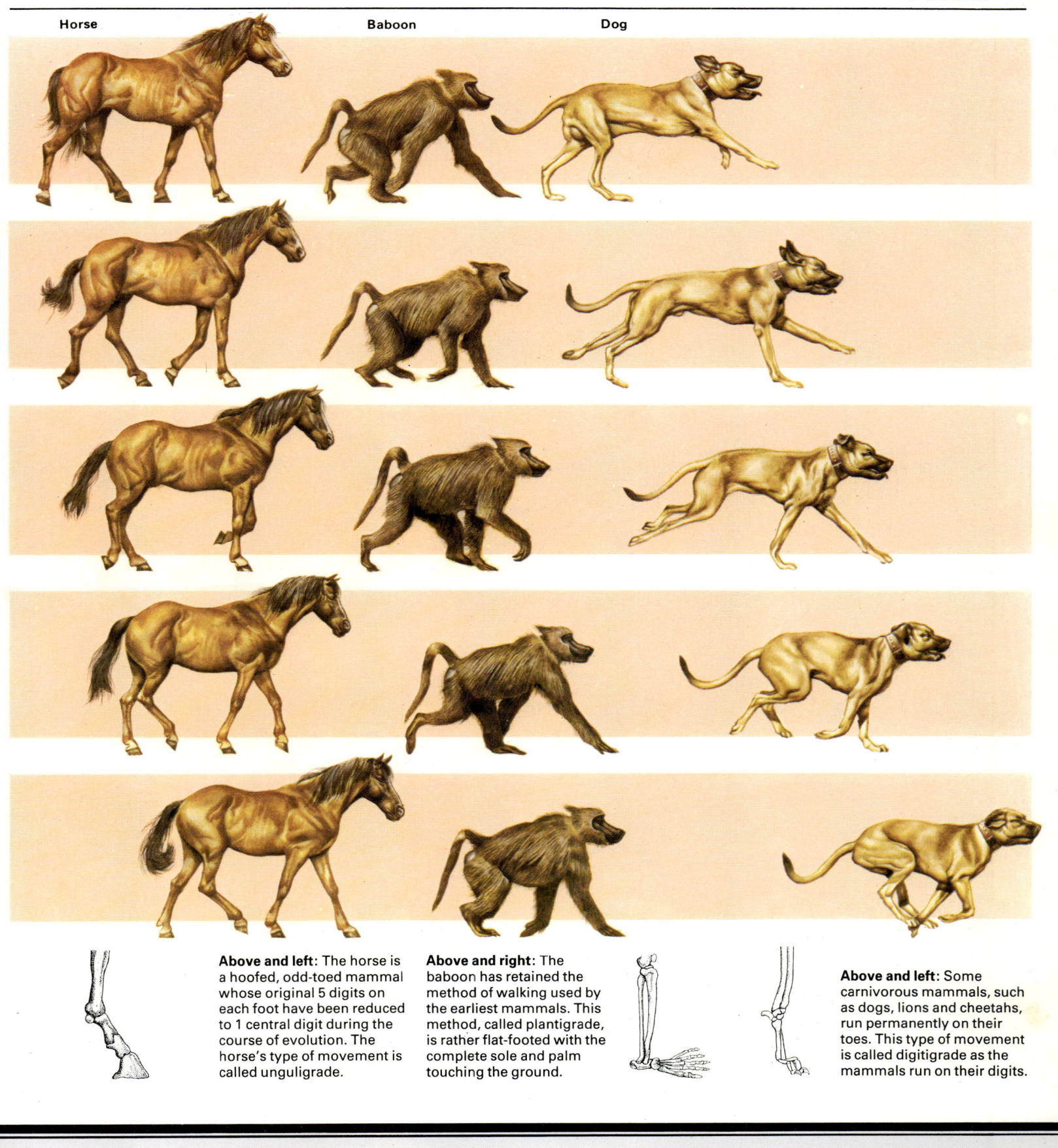

Mammals 11

Horse   Baboon   Dog

Above and left: The horse is a hoofed, odd-toed mammal whose original 5 digits on each foot have been reduced to 1 central digit during the course of evolution. The horse's type of movement is called unguligrade.

Above and right: The baboon has retained the method of walking used by the earliest mammals. This method, called plantigrade, is rather flat-footed with the complete sole and palm touching the ground.

Above and left: Some carnivorous mammals, such as dogs, lions and cheetahs, run permanently on their toes. This type of movement is called digitigrade as the mammals run on their digits.

tains the WHALES, DOLPHINS and porpoises. They are all highly adapted for an aquatic life. They use their forelimbs as paddles, have no hind-limbs and their tail is a pair of horizontal fins.
Chimpanzees are APES that inhabit the forests of Africa, living in family groups. They sleep at night in trees and are inoffensive unless molested.
Chiroptera. This order contains the BATS.

D Deer are all ARTIODACTYLS and the group includes species such as fallow, red, Virginian and mule deer as well as moose, CARIBOU and reindeer. Most have bony antlers (usually only the males) which are shed every year.
Dermoptera, see FLYING LEMUR.
Dog refers to either the 130 domesticated breeds or to the wild species which include the WOLF, FOX and JACKAL of the family Canidae.
Dolphins are apparently highly intelligent CETACEANS. They are often seen in family groups, or 'schools', playing at the ocean's surface and following ships.
Dugongs live in the Red Sea and Indian Ocean and are members of the order Sirenia. Seal-like in shape, they are slow-moving, timid mammals that feed on seaweeds.

E Echidnas, or spiny ANTEATERS, are termite-eating MONOTREMES from Australia and New Guinea. Their long, beak-like muzzle probes for food. The upper parts of the body are covered with a mixture of spines and hair.
Edentata. This order includes the SLOTHS, ANTEATERS and ARMADILLOS, all of which live in the Americas.
Elephants are the largest living land mammals of the order Proboscidea. There are 2 species, the African and the Indian or Asian. Their trunk is used for feeding, drinking and bathing. The African elephant has the longer tusks and larger ears.

Young chimpanzee

Porcupine

12 Mammals

Above and left: Carnivores (the meat-eaters) such as the lionesses illustrated here, have dagger-like canine teeth for piercing and tearing the prey, with slicing cheek teeth that cut the meat into lumps.

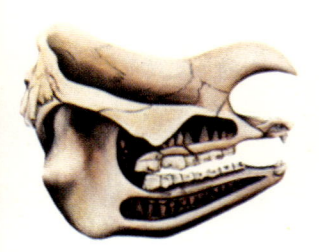

Above and left: Herbivores (the plant eaters) such as the white rhinoceros seen here, have to eat large quantities of plants daily to obtain enough energy for survival. The cheek teeth grind down the plant material.

Above and left: A giant anteater rips open a termite nest using its strong front claws. Then the long, sticky, extensible tongue laps up the insects. No teeth are required for this diet.

in size to the rodents and flourishes in every part of the world except the polar regions. The bat flies using wings that have evolved from the five-fingered forelimbs — webs of naked skin stretching between the digits and usually enveloping the hind legs and part of the tail. Although some mammals are given the term 'flying', such as the FLYING LEMUR and flying squirrel, these mammals actually can only passively glide or parachute on outstretched webbed limbs down to a lower level in the trees.

Feeding and senses of mammals

Mammals, being warm-blooded and with a high energy use, need a certain amount of food in order to keep the body processes functioning correctly. The plant eaters, or herbivores, do not need to use up much energy searching for food. However, winter, drought, or severe climatic changes, may make this food source scarce and so the mammal has to search harder. Another difficulty with this type of diet is that not much energy is obtained from plant material. This means that considerable amounts must be eaten by the mammal to stay alive. An adult African bull elephant, using its trunk to push leaves and branches into its mouth, will consume about 150 kilograms of vegetation a day. Herbivores must have flat, ridged teeth in order to grind down the tough plant material before swallowing.

Certain herbivorous mammals, such as the elephant, TAPIR and giraffe, browse on bushes and trees while many others feed on grasses. The latter species includes BISON, antelopes, white RHINOCEROSES and deer. The gerenuk of Africa is sometimes called the giraffe antelope because it has a long thin neck. If it cannot reach high leaves it will stand on its hind legs to eat.

The members of the RODENT order, some 1,700 species, are basically vegetarians. They all have huge front teeth for biting and nibbling plant matter and powerful grinding cheek teeth.

The CARNIVORES, or flesh-eaters, are those that prey on other animals. These include the large cats, wild dogs, weasels, foxes, and seals. All flesh-eaters have piercing canine teeth, and slicing and cutting cheek teeth. Shrews are also carnivorous but as they eat mainly insects are termed INSECTIVORES.

The fastest land mammal, the cheetah, stealthily tracks its prey, such as a gazelle or antelope,

---

F Flying lemurs, or colugos, are the only species of the order Dermoptera. Cat-sized with large eyes, they do not fly but glide using a membrane which extends round its arms, legs and tail. They range from Indo-China to the Philippines.
Foxes are widespread. Their habitat ranges from the Arctic to the North African deserts. The European red fox has, in recent years, invaded the outskirts of towns to obtain food.

African elephant

G Gerbils, or sand rats, come from the drier parts of Africa and Asia. Nocturnal, burrowing, seed-eating RODENTS, they are now very popular children's pets.
Gibbons are the smallest APES and come from south-east Asia. Living in family groups, they are expert climbers, hooking their long fingers over branches and swinging along hand over hand.
Giraffes are ARTIODACTYLS found only in Africa. They have long legs and can outrun a horse. Using their elongated neck, they browse on acacia trees in the dry savanna areas south of the Sahara desert.
Gnu, or wildebeeste, are common antelopes of the East African plains. They have a buffalo-like head and horns, with a mane and tail like a horse.

Ibex

Goats. Species in the wild include ibexes and markhors. Wild goats of Europe live on steep and rocky upland areas and are usually extremely wary of man.
Gorillas are the largest APES. They live in family groups in tropical Africa. Inoffensive unless molested, they feed on leaves, vegetables and fruit. Old males attain almost 2 metres in height and 200 kg in weight.

H Hamsters are RODENTS often kept as pets. In western Europe they live in underground tunnels and

Mammals 13

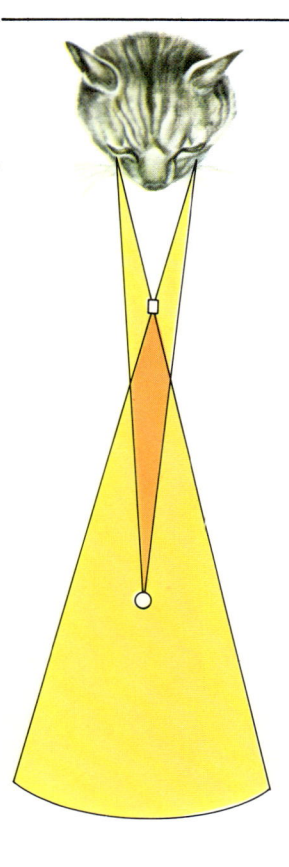

Right: Just as echo-sounding is used by ships to find the depth of the ocean, dolphins and most bats have evolved a similar mechanism to find their way about and detect prey. Short pulses of sound, far beyond the limit of human hearing, are emitted by the mammal. These bounce off objects such as insects or fishes, creating echoes. The brain can interpret the echoes to locate prey or avoid obstacles.

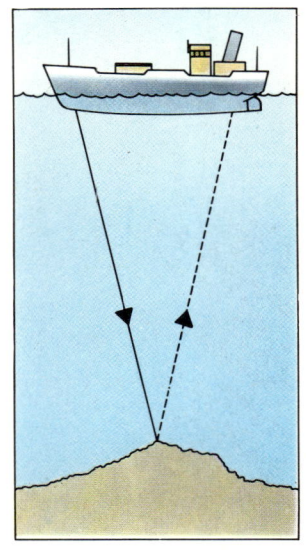

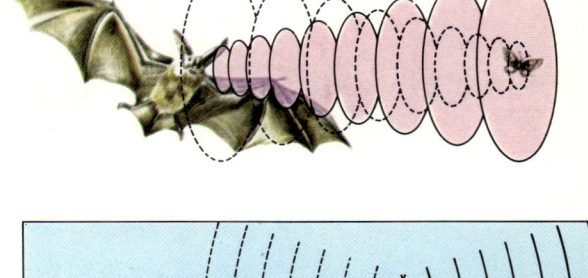

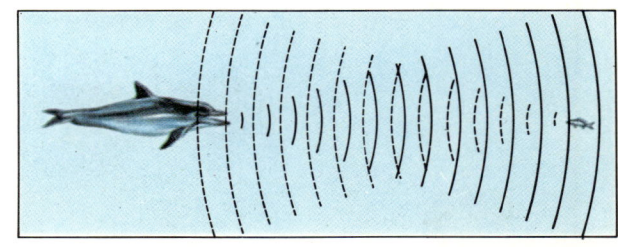

Above: Forwards facing eyes give overlapping, or binocular, vision. The animal sees 2 images of the same subject and can focus well. Thus a cat can judge the distance to jump when moving about from branch to branch.

Above: A tiger marks his territory by spraying scent from an anal gland over shrubs along his invisible territorial boundary. The scent warns other tigers that they are entering someone else's territory.

and then attacks swiftly, leaping and grabbing its victim when within reach. It kills quickly by biting the victim's neck so that the vital jugular artery that goes to the brain is severed. In a pride of lions, the females often hunt in a group, ambushing prey such as ZEBRA, gnu or antelope.

The carnivores of the sea are the seals, sealions and certain CETACEANS such as dolphins and killer whales. Depending on the mammal, the prey ranges from shrimps and crabs to penguins and large fishes.

The mixed feeders, or omnivores, are a successful group because they will eat almost anything they can find. The brown bear will eat meat such as salmon or deer when it is available. However, it will happily consume large amounts of fruit, insects, roots, and grasses in its diet.

If a mammal is preyed upon by others it usually has large ears and eyes positioned on the side of the head so that it can hear and see predators before they get too close. A giraffe has the added advantage of being very tall and grassland animals, such as antelopes, gnu and gazelles, will often will be found grazing nearby. They can thus benefit from their living lookout tower.

Some mammals have eyes facing forwards so that the vision in each eye overlaps to give binocular vision. They are usually either hunters or tree-dwellers. This type of vision allows the animal to judge distances so that, for example, it helps a CHIMPANZEE to swing between branches.

Smells and scents are very important in mammals to bring the sexes together for mating, or to keep unwanted visitors away. Many mammals have large, moist noses (rhinaria) to detect other scents in the air. The skunk has special scent glands near its tail which squirt out an evil-smelling fluid over the advancing enemy, allowing the skunk to escape during the confusion. Other animals such as wild cats, dogs, musk deer, red PANDAS and HIPPOPOTAMUSES use scents to mark out their territories.

A very special type of hearing is called echolocation. This system works rather like radar. The mammal emits high-frequency noises which are bounced back to it off objects in its path. BATS echolocate in the air and dolphins find their way underwater by this method.

---

collect plant food in their cheek pouches. The golden hamster is smaller than the common hamster. The golden hamsters which we now have as pets, all originate from 1 female and 12 young caught in Syria in 1930.
Hippopotamuses are large ARTIODACTYLS distantly related to pigs. They live a semi-aquatic life in the rivers of Africa. They feed on land during the night, returning to the cooler water by day.

I Insectivora. This order contains some 285 species of small, primitive mammals. Most members, such as the shrews and tenrecs, have long snouts and feed on insects.

Hedgehog

J Jackals are members of the dog family and find much of their food by scavenging. Most species are a little larger than foxes and are found in Africa, south-east Europe and Asia.
Jaguars are large cats from South America about the same size as LEOPARDS but heavier in build. They also have a spotted coat, though the spots are larger and have dark centres. Their favourite prey is capybara, a large rodent.

K Kangaroos live only in Australia and are MARSUPIALS. Great grey and red kangaroos attain up to 2 metres in height and weigh up to 70 kg. They are capable of 40 km per hour and leaps of 8 metres are not uncommon.
Koalas are small, bear-like MARSUPIALS with tufted ears and a prominent snout. Although looking like teddy bears, they have aggressive natures. They feed only on the leaves of eucalyptus (gum) trees and are now protected species.

L Lagomorpha. This order contains the rabbits, hares and pikas.
Lemurs are small rare PRIMATES that live on the island of Madagascar. They have a fox-like muzzle, very big

Mammals

shown by other members of the family.

The period of development of a mammal inside the mother's body is called the gestation period. This length of time varies with the species, the larger animals generally having the longest development periods. An elephant is born after about 22 months. The young of the pouched mammals (MARSUPIALS) are born after a very short gestation period. The American OPOSSUM young are born after 12 or 13 days' development and at birth are no bigger than a honeybee. Although from eight to 18 young are born, less than seven survive the period of further development in their mother's pouch. They remain there for 60 to 70 days attached to, and sucking from, the nipples and then begin to move about her body and accept solid food. The KOALA and the red KANGAROO both have a gestation period of about a month.

The egg-laying MONOTREMES have no nipples.

Left: A red fox vixen offers warmth, protection and milk to her young cubs. At birth these babies are quite helpless.

Below: In the pouched mammals, like this koala, the young are born early but are strong enough to crawl into the mother's pouch.

Reproduction and growth

During the breeding season males and females use various methods of courtship prior to mating and producing a family. Quite often the males live separate lives to the females, but during an annual breeding season they establish a breeding range or territory. For example, the red DEER stag marks out his area using a scent gland, gathers several hinds into his herd and keeps a watch out for any intruding males. If another stag enters his territory, the occupying stag will attempt to see him off with loud roars or actual combat with his fine set of antlers. These antlers are grown during the earlier months and lost after the rutting season (when the deer are sexually active).

The mammal with the largest harem is the fur seal bull, who may tend and guard more than 100 cows, although the number is usually between 40 and 60.

Some mammals live as family groups, such as the LIONS, gorillas and baboons. This has the advantage that a partner is always available for the mating season. When the baby is born, although the mother gives the youngster milk, warmth, care and affection, parental care is also

---

eyes and a long tail (except for the indri).
Lemmings are furry, stocky rodents of the tundra regions of the Northern Hemisphere. Every 4-5 years, when there are too many animals for the food available, they migrate in vast numbers. The majority die on the way.
Leopards are large wild spotted cats that range from Africa east to China, with black varieties (black panthers) being frequently found. Excellent climbers, they usually drag prey up into a tree 'larder' where it is safe from other predators.
Lions are mainly found in Africa but a few live in the Gir forest of India. The male has a shaggy mane and heads the family group known as a pride. The females will often ambush their prey at a waterhole; zebra and antelope being favoured.
Llamas are the South American relatives of CAMELS, but are humpless, smaller, and very woolly. Found only in a domestic state, like the alpaca, they are bred for their fine fur.

M **Marsupialia.** This order contains all the pouched mammals (e.g. KANGAROOS) of Australia and Central and South America. Embryo-like young are born after a short gestation period and continue their development in the mother's pouch until fully formed.
Moles are underground burrowers of the order INSECTIVORA. Their forelimbs have large digging claws. The ears and eyes are small, the body cylindrical, and the fur is usually black.
Monkeys are agile PRIMATES that are highly adapted for a tree-dwelling life, except the ground-dwelling BABOONS. Most have gripping hands, binocular vision and tails which act as balancing organs. New World species have prehensile tails.

Monotremata. This order contains the egg-laying mammals (duck-billed platypus and the ECHIDNA).

O **Opossums** are marsupials found in America and Australia. The American common opossum is cat-sized and rather rat-like in appearance. They are nocturnal and expert climbers.
Orang-utans are slow, heavily-built primates from the jungles of Sumatra and Borneo. They have naked faces with long, reddish hair over the rest of body. The old males grow large swel-

Jaguar

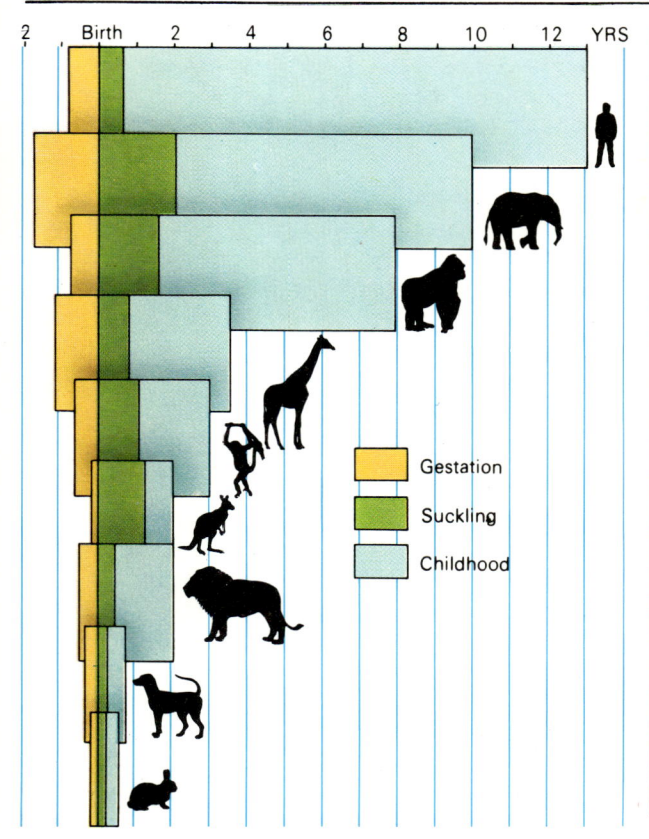

When a duck-billed platypus has laid her two tiny eggs in an underground nest she incubates them for about two weeks. On hatching, the naked, blind babies feed on the milk which comes onto the mother's belly from mammary pores.

Most mammals give birth to fully developed young, but they are smaller than the adult mammals and rather helpless. These are the 'placental mammals', and include cats, dogs, horses, antelopes and bears. The mother feeds her offspring on her nourishing milk and the amount of care and attention depends on the youngster's development.

GERBILS, kittens and fox cubs are just some of the young that are born blind, naked and helpless. The mother takes great care of them, feeding, cleaning, protecting and keeping them warm. Sometimes she brings her offspring up entirely alone, the father having gone back to living a 'bachelor' life.

Some mammals are able to walk and look after themselves almost as soon as they are born. For instance, a young antelope or gazelle born on the African plain can usually stand and walk within half an hour of birth. Like all mammals it instinctively knows where to find its mother's milk. After feeding it moves off with its mother to rejoin the herd, and it can keep up with the moving herd within a few hours of birth. This is most important, as hunting hyenas, JACKALS, or lions are always on the lookout for strays.

Above left: The chart compares rates at which different mammals mature and shows the relative duration of gestation (the period within the mother's body), suckling (the length of time until weaning), and childhood (the time taken to achieve sexual maturity). In general, the larger the animal the longer the gestation period, except in marsupials, such as the kangaroo, where the baby is born at an early stage in development.

Above right: A 12-day-old rabbit leaves its warren for the first time. Although blind and naked at birth, its development is rapid and it soon leads an independent life. Other mammals have much longer periods of growing up.

Social life

Within a family group, such as a pride of lions or baboon troop, there are various rules which all the members follow. Usually, each group has a leader. This is a large lion in a pride, or a fit, aggressive, male baboon in a troop. In a herd of elephants, however, it is quite often an old female, as adult bulls are not allowed within certain elephant herds except during the breeding season. Below the leader every member learns his place so that a hierarchy is set up. In a baboon troop, social grooming is an act of behaviour that not only is a form of hygiene but maintains friendly social relations within the group.

Certain mammals migrate on a large scale but the numbers are few compared with the hundreds of species of birds that migrate annually.

---

lings on the face and throat.

Pandas. There are 2 species. The large, bear-like giant panda of the bamboo forests of China and the cat-like red panda of the mountain forests of western China and the eastern Himalayas. Both are related to RACCOONS. The giant panda feeds almost entirely on bamboo.
Pangolins, see PHOLIDOTA.
Perissodactyla. This order of odd-toed ungulates includes horses, RHINOCEROSES and TAPIRS. They are 1- or 3-toed.

Pholidota. This order contains the African and Asian pangolins. They are toothless ANTEATERS with the upper body and tail covered with horny, overlapping scales, and large digging claws on their forefeet. They roll into a ball for defence.
Pinnipedia. This order contains the SEALS and walruses. Their flippers are limbs modified for an aquatic life. On land they move clumsily but they only come ashore once a year to breed.
Porcupines are large rodents found in North America, Africa and Asia. Their body hairs have evolved into sharp quills which give an effective defence against enemies.
Primates. This order contains tree shrews, lemurs, MONKEYS, APES and man. The brain is usually well-developed and the limbs are usually long with 5 fingers or toes. The thumb and big toe (except in man) are opposable for grasping. Social life is well developed.
Proboscidea, see ELEPHANTS.

Racoons are nocturnal American mammals recognized by their black and white ringed tail and black 'face mask'. Vegetables and aquatic animals are 'washed' with the forefeet before being eaten.

Racoon

Reindeer is another name for the CARIBOU but usually refers to Eurasian species.
Rhinoceroses are large, thick-skinned PERISSODACTYLS that are inoffensive and retiring in spite of their appearance. They are largely solitary creatures. Five species exist: the Indian, Javan, Sumatran, white and black.
Rodentia. This order contains gnawing animals such as rats, mice, porcupines, beavers and voles. All have a single pair of chisel-like incisors, which grow continually but are kept in check by continual use.

Mammals

Above: A herd of wildebeeste are here seen crossing a wide river in Tanzania on their annual migration in search of fresh grazing and water.
Right: A dormouse has retired to its sleeping quarters by mid-October. Curled up into a ball to conserve heat, its body metabolism slows down until the warmer weather arrives.
Below: Hamadryas baboons here indulge in a mutual grooming session. This activity helps to strengthen social bonds between various members of the primate troop.

Like birds, mammals migrate mainly to find a better climate, fresh food supplies or to their annual breeding grounds. The migratory instinct is in most cases a combination of these reasons.

Land mammals face many barriers on their journeys — mountains, deserts and rivers being the major obstacles. In Africa up until the present century, antelopes, gazelles, gnu and elephants used to make annual journeys in herds of sometimes many thousands of animals. As a result of hunting by man, these magnificent sights have almost vanished. Gnu still make annual cycles following regular trails in search of grass and water as the dry season progresses. In North America the caribou still migrate in a regimented procession, travelling along established routes to destinations some 1,300 kilometres from their summer feeding and breeding grounds on the high barren ranges of the Arctic tundra. They usually move at six or seven kilometres an hour until they reach the wooded areas of the taiga (a region between the tundra and steppe), where they feed on lichens and the buds and shoots of trees. The caribou of northern Siberia (known there as reindeer) also migrate but they live today in a semi-domesticated state. Man has adopted a nomadic lifestyle in order to follow the mammal that gives him milk, flesh and hide.

There are many species of bat that make seasonal migrations. They have few barriers to face, except for bad weather and wide stretches of sea. In the oceans, whales travel thousands of kilometres annually. The whalebone whales feed mainly on plankton, especially krill (small shrimp-like crustaceans), whereas the toothed whales feed on fish. The summer is spent feeding on shoals of these plankton and fish in the cold waters of the Antarctic. In winter they migrate to warm tropical waters where the young are born.

Some mammals do not migrate when the frosts and snows of winter begin and food becomes very scarce. Instead, they feed almost continuously through the summer months, putting on thick layers of insulating and energy-giving fat. Then they find a suitable dry, draught-free spot, and curl up and sleep until the warmth of spring awakes them. This is known as hibernation and dormice, some bats, hedgehogs, ground squirrels and HAMSTERS are all mammals that go into a deep sleep during the winter.

Seals are aquatic mammals of the order PINNIPEDIA, mainly living in northern waters and in Antarctica. Seals come ashore for breeding, with up to 50 cows forming a harem ruled over by an old bull.
Sirenia. This order contains the manatees, and DUGONGS (sea-cows).
Sloths are very slow members of the order EDENTATA. They live in trees where they hang upside down from branches using their long curved claws. They mainly feed on leaves of the Cecropia tree in South America.

Tapirs are donkey-sized, stoutly-built PERISSODACTYLS found in Malaya and South America. The snout is extended into a short trunk which is used for browsing on foliage.
Tigers are large cats found from India to China and Malaya. The striped reddish and black coat helps to camouflage them in their jungle home. Their diet varies from small game to large animals such as water buffalo. When food is short, or they are injured, they may become man-eaters.
Tubulidentata, see AARDVARK.

Wallabies are small Australian KANGAROOS. Many were formerly hunted for their valuable pelts.
Whales belong to the order CETACEA. They are divided into the toothless whales (blue, humpback) that feed on plankton and the toothed species (DOLPHINS, porpoises) that feed mainly on fish.
Wolves are wild dogs of the order CARNIVORA that hunt in packs.

Zebras are striped horses of the order PERISSODACTYLA. Three species (mountain, common, and Grévy's) are all found in Africa south of the Sahara. Herds will visit waterholes at dawn and dusk, ever watchful for prowling lions or leopards.

Burchell's zebra

The ancestors of birds were toothed reptiles, but their modern descendants are fully adapted to life in the air, with light bones and streamlined bodies. The annual migrations of some birds are still not fully understood by man.

Birds

Birds are more numerous than mammals, the only other warm-blooded group of animals living today. There are over 8,500 species of birds in existence, but only 4,200 species of mammals. Their success is due mainly to the fact that they can fly. Most species have retained the use of flight but several (PENGUINS, OSTRICHES) have adapted to other methods.

The main identifying feature of a bird is its feathers. Feathers evolved from the scales of reptiles and are the key to their success. They grow from the bird's skin as hair or fingernails grow on humans. However, feathers grow to a definite size and then stop. Although they are firmly fixed in the skin, they suffer from wear and tear, so they are renewed every so often by a process called moulting. Old feathers are usually shed once a year, with new ones growing in their place. This usually happens immediately after the breeding season.

Feathers are vital for many reasons. They trap an insulating layer of air next to the body so that the high body temperature remains constant. Many feathers are brilliantly coloured and play an important part in the bird's social life. The feathers also help to give the bird its streamlined shape and the long, strong tail and wing feathers provide the flight surfaces.

The skeleton of a bird is as light as possible. The bones are hollow and some are fused together to give greater strength. If a bird had to carry its young within its body, then there would be times when it would be too heavy to fly. So the birds retain the egg-laying habits of their reptilian ancestors. An egg is laid usually within 24 hours of fertilization.

The legs of birds are adapted for walking or swimming, depending on the species, and are also important shock absorbers for when the bird lands. To maintain the centre of gravity, the thighs are held close to the body, the knees

Below: Feathers are unique to birds. Their major functions are to help in flight and provide body insulation. The wings evolved from reptilian forelimbs some 150 million years ago. Massive pectoral muscles are attached to the deep breastbone. These provide the power to move the wings.

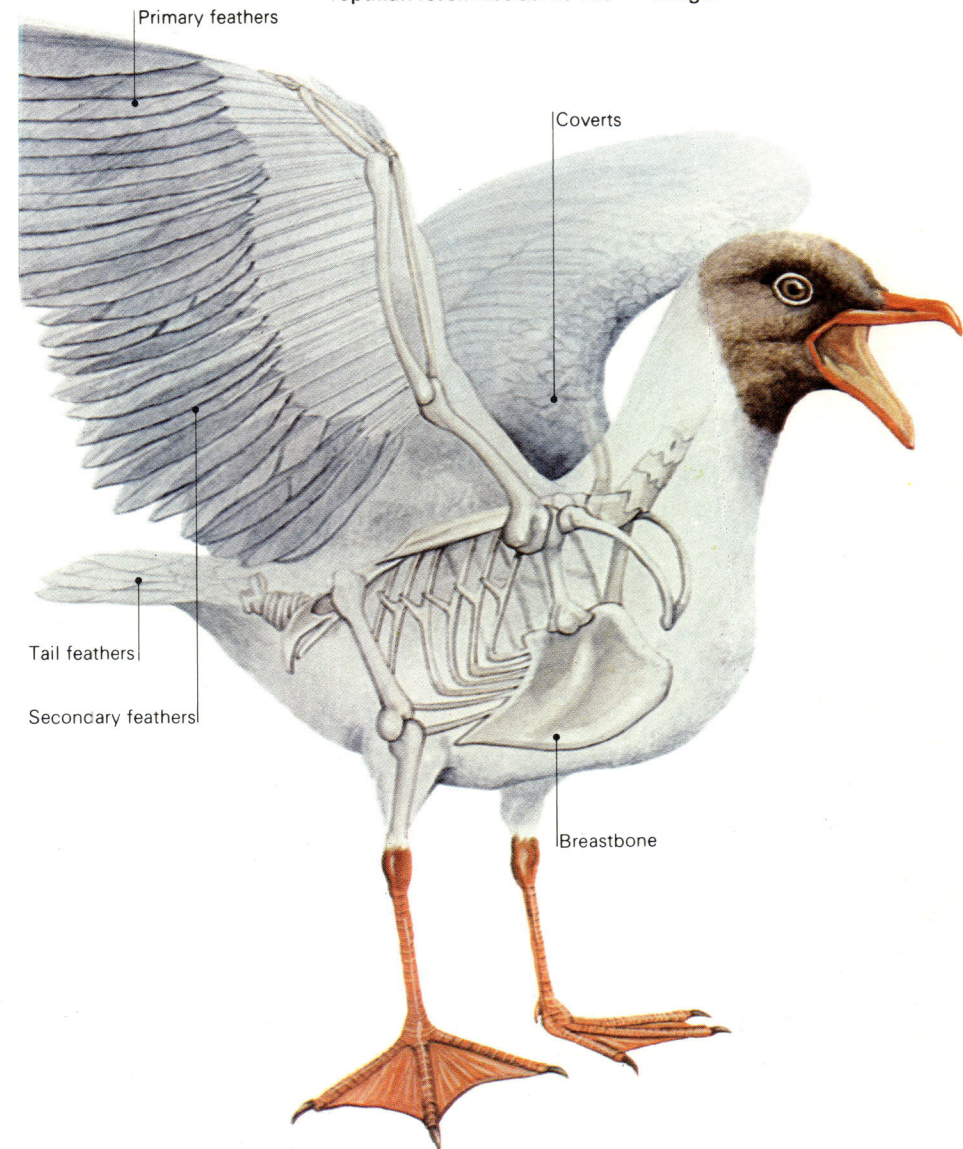

Reference

A Albatrosses are graceful oceanic sea birds. Their very long narrow wings make them excellent fliers and gliders. They land on oceanic islands only to breed.
Anhingas, or snakebirds, are slender long-necked birds that spear their prey. They throw their victim into the air and catch it so that the head is swallowed first.
Avocets are black and white slender waders with a long up-curved bill which is used to find molluscs, crustaceans and insects in shallow water.
B Bee-eaters are brightly-coloured birds of temperate and tropical parts of Eurasia, Africa and Australia. Some species rub the dead bee against a branch to remove its sting. Most nest in colonies in sand banks.
Birds of paradise are found in Australasia. The males are very brightly coloured and are famous for their displays where they dance, pose and hang upside down.

Birds of prey is a term given to all birds, not necessarily related, that are flesh-eaters. They include OWLS, EAGLES, and VULTURES.

Avocet

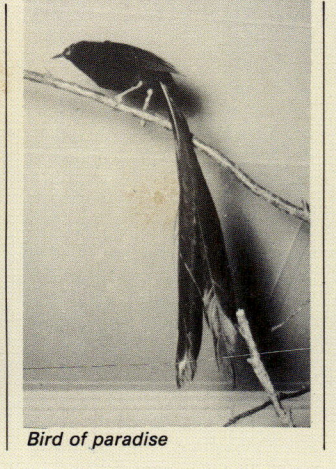

Bird of paradise

Blackbirds are members of the THRUSH family. Males have a golden bill with dull black plumage. Females are dark brown with a dull orange bill. The name is also given to American birds of the troupial family.
Bobolinks are American blackbirds famous for their migrations. They leave their lush summer northern farmland homes to winter on the pampas of Argentina.
Bowerbirds are less gaudy relatives of the BIRDS OF PARADISE and live in Australia and New Guinea. The males build strange display struc-

Right: The sulphur-crested cockatoo propels itself by the large primary feathers controlled by the 'hand' part of each wing. The secondary feathers and the inner part of the wing maintain lift, while the downstroke is the power stroke. Then the feathers are closed flat so as to encounter the maximum amount of air resistance.

usually hidden beneath feathers. The leg's visible joint is actually the ankle, the bird being raised up on its toes. The majority of birds, such as the perching birds or passerines, have four toes, one pointing backwards and three forwards.

How birds fly

The ability to fly has caused most birds to be designed on a general uniform body plan. However, there is an enormous range in size, from the tiny HUMMINGBIRDS to the largest fliers, the kori bustards. The even bigger EMUS, CASSOWARIES and OSTRICHES are flightless.

The wings of a bird have evolved from the front limbs of its reptilian ancestors. They are streamlined to cut through the air with very little resistance. The shape of the wings vary, depending on the lifestyle of the bird.

Certain birds rely on winds and air currents to soar and glide for long periods. Birds that soar over the land include the VULTURES, EAGLES, kites and HAWKS. They have long, broad wings and can go very high using thermal currents (hot air pockets). Over the ocean the finest soarers are the ALBATROSSES, FRIGATE BIRDS, shearwaters and GULLS. They have light, long, narrow wings that enable them to glide for long periods without flapping their wings. They steer using their tail feathers, and tip their wings and body to bank in turns like an aircraft.

In flapping flight the power comes mainly from the downstroke and from the primary feathers which grow at the tips of the wings. They act on rather the same principle as propellers of a propeller-driven aeroplane. The sequence can be seen in the frame by frame illustrations at the top of these pages. Strong flapping flight is seen in birds, such as GEESE, HERONS, STORKS, CORMORANTS, THRUSHES and most FINCHES.

The aerial acrobats are the tiny humming-

---

tures which they decorate with flowers. They dance in these 'bowers' to attract a mate. When mated, the female goes off to lay her eggs and raise the young alone.

Buzzards are some 26 species of birds grouped in the HAWK family. All are hunters, feeding largely on reptiles, amphibians and small mammals.

Canaries are small domesticated FINCHES that originally lived wild in the Canary Islands.

Cassowaries are timid, large flightless birds of the Australasian tropical forests. If attacked they kick with their long legs and sharp claws. A bony helmet, or casque, protects their head as they run through the forest.

Chickens are the domesticated form of the wild jungle fowl from southern Asia. By selective breeding a great variety have been produced. Leghorns, Andalusian and Sussex are just some of the breeds.

Cockatoos are members of the PARROT family. They differ from other parrots in having a crest of long, pointed feathers that they can raise and lower at will. They are found in Australasia where they live in noisy flocks.

Condors are very large American vultures. They have a thick, hooked bill and a bare head and neck. The Californian condor is today one of the rarest birds.

Cormorants are quite large black sea birds with long bodies. They have large webbed feet and a long neck with a slightly hooked bill. They dive underwater to catch fish and can remain submerged for up to a minute. The Japanese train cormorants to catch fish.

Crossbills are small seed-eating FINCHES. The birds' powerful beak can exert 100lb/in^2 at the cutting edge

Cormorant

and can cut through the hard outer case of coniferous seed cones with ease.

Crows are bold, noisy and aggressive birds. Their close

Crossbill

Birds 19

Left: A barn owl returning with a field mouse. The soft plumage helps to make its flight virtually silent.

Above: A hummingbird can fly in almost any direction. Its most remarkable feat is that of hovering.

Below: Warm air rises from the hot land and expands. Cold air rushes in and creates a rising hot air bubble. A vulture uses these thermal air currents to gain height.

Below: An albatross has a wingspan of over 3.5 metres. Its long, narrow wings are adapted for gliding flight over the southern oceans.

birds. They can fly backwards as well as forwards, vertically and stop abruptly to hover. The secret of this bird's success is that the wing is held almost rigid and revolves on a swivel joint at the shoulder. The wing moves swiftly back and forth instead of whirling around like the rotary blades of a helicopter.

Some birds combine flapping and gliding flight. Ibises flap their wings a few times then glide a little farther before flapping once more. WOODPECKERS also do this and their flight pattern is a wavy line. The hummingbirds have the fastest wingbeats per second (over 80) of any bird. They are also fast fliers, up to 95 kilometres per hour by the ruby-throated hummingbird.

Certain other birds can also hover and the technique is usually used to spy for food. A NIGHTJAR will hover for just a few seconds, while a KESTREL has perfected this technique and will hover above a grass verge or meadow waiting for a small rodent to emerge from cover.

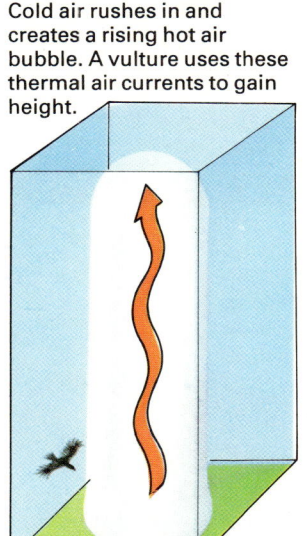

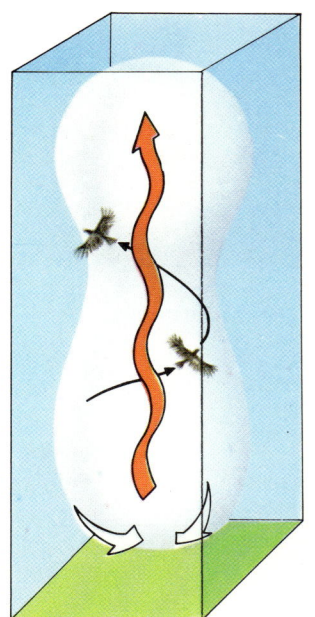

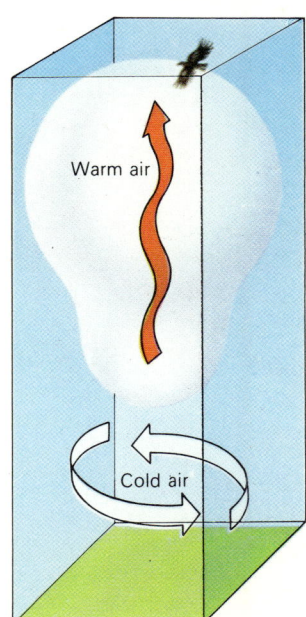

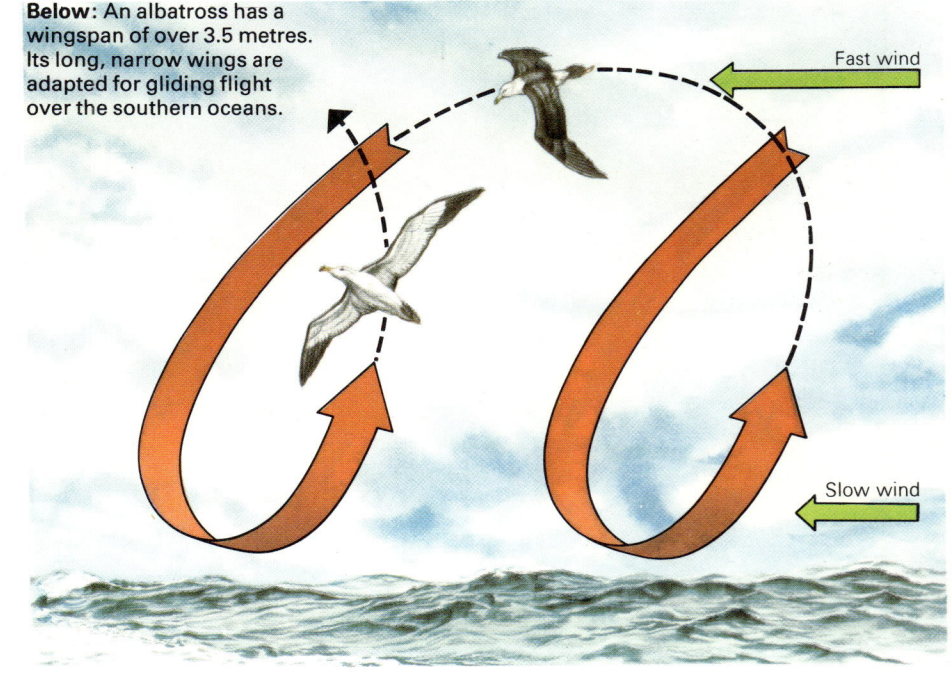

---

relatives are the ravens, rooks, jackdaws and the more colourful jays.
Cuckoos are famous for being parasitic birds. The female lays her eggs in other birds' nests. She is even capable of producing an egg which matches those of the host species. On hatching, the chick usually pushes any of the host's eggs or nestlings out of the nest. It thus enjoys all the attention of its foster parents. Most species are migratory.
Curlews are brown birds with long legs and a long, curved bill. Curlews often frequent dry uplands, feeding on berries, seeds and insects. They also probe coastal marshes and mud flats for worms.

Golden eagle

E Eagles are large hawks, and are fine fliers and soarers. They prey on small mammals, birds and amphibians. Nests, called eyries, are often found high up on cliffs. Their hooked bills and huge talons tear their victims to pieces. The golden eagle is perhaps the best known and is found in mountainous areas across Eurasia and North America.
Emus are large flightless birds, related to the CASSOWARY. They are widespread in savannah areas of Australia, feeding mainly on vegetable matter.

F Falcons are usually solitary birds of prey. Their flight pattern is direct and swift, live prey usually being caught with the talons.
Finches are small, tree-loving, basically seed-eating birds. They are found almost worldwide.
Flamingoes are large water birds that stand over a metre high. They have very long legs, a long neck, and a unique filter-feeding bill. The plumage varies from pale to deep pink. They breed in colonies, each pair constructing a mud nest.
Flycatchers are a large insect-eating family of perching birds. The 350 species, usually called tyrant flycatchers, hunt in the open, catching insects in flight.
Frigate birds are about a metre long and have the largest wing area, in proportion to body weight, of any bird. The wingspan can be up to 2·4 metres. Their plumage is black, the male having a scarlet inflatable throat sac.
Frogmouths are small grey-brown patterned birds that range from India to Australia. The short, broad flat bill has a hooked tip and

Birds

Feet and beaks for food

A bird's beak enables it to eat, defend itself, build a nest and preen its feathers. However, the shape of the beak, or bill, is usually designed to deal with the type of food eaten by the species and to enable the bird to reach its particular type of food. The fact that birds, particularly finches, have bills adapted to suit the food available to them was first noted by Darwin in 1835 on the Galapagos Islands.

Seed-eaters, such as SPARROWS, CHICKENS and certain finches, have cone-shaped bills. The sharp point picks up the seeds and the rest of the bill crushes them. A crossbill is well-named as its scissors-like beak can open pine cones.

Left: A sulphur-breasted toucan displays its huge, colourful beak. The beak is made lighter by being honey combed with air chambers.

Below: The frogmouth's wide gaping beak has sensitive bristles that enable it to trap insects on the wing during the night.

Below: The mallard's broad bill has fringes which sift out tiny animals and plants from the water.

Below: The macaw's hooked bill is a powerful and efficient nutcracker. After the case is cracked the tongue extracts the fruit.

Below: The down-curved, long, slim bill of the Kiwi is used to probe the ground for worms. The nostrils at its tip also help to locate food.

Below: The bent bill of the flamingo filters out mud and water, but retains the minute plants and animals for food.

Above: The frogmouth's feet are designed for perching on a branch. Its body plumage usually blends in perfectly with the surroundings.

Above: The webbing between the mallard's front 3 toes gives the duck's foot propulsion through the water.

Above: To help with climbing trees and gripping, the macaw has 2 toes pointing forwards and 2 backwards.

Above: In this flightless bird, the hind toe is greatly reduced. The feet are sturdily built for running.

Above: The flamingo's webbed feet are adapted for wading in mud without sinking, and also for propulsion when swimming.

---

opens to a huge gape — hence the name. They catch insects in flight.

G **Geese** are large aquatic birds of the duck family. The best known North American species is the Canada goose, with its black neck and head.

Grebes are long, sleek water birds found almost worldwide. They are famous for their courtship displays. They usually ride high in the water with their long, thin neck outstretched.

Grouse are game birds of the order Galliformes. The largest is the capercaillie of the Eurasian evergreen forests. The metre-long black male extends his tail into a fan when displaying.

Willow grouse

They eat conifer shoots and buds. Ptarmigan are small grouse.

Gulls are long-winged web-footed water birds found throughout the world. Though often spoken of as 'seagulls', they do not venture far out to sea. They will eat almost anything.

H **Hawks** are some 40 species of sharp-clawed, long-shanked, fast fliers of the FALCON order. They live mainly on small mammals and birds.

Herons are long-legged, long-necked water birds with broad, rounded wings and fairly short tails. Unlike the STORKS and FLAMINGOES, their head is completely feathered. They also carry their necks kinked into an S-shape when flying and at rest due to the length of their neck vertebrae.

Hummingbirds are tiny, fast-flying American birds. Over 300 species are known. They have slender, pointed bills with fringe-tipped tongues that can be projected beyond the beak tip.

K **Kestrels** are small FALCONS, distributed over all the continents except Antarctica. They are noted for the ability to hover on gently flapping wings while scanning the ground for small

Heron

Nightjars, SWIFTS and FROGMOUTHS have tiny beaks but their gaping mouths are enormous and enable them to catch insects in flight. Members of the parrot family have beaks that act as both nutcrackers and fruit spoons. Eagles and other birds of prey have hook-shaped upper bills that tear their victims to pieces.

Ducks are often termed dabblers because they use their broad, flat bills to dabble in the water and mud to find worms and other aquatic animals. Any sand or dirt is sieved out by the serrated tongue and lower bill. An extreme example of a filtering beak is seen in the FLAMINGOES. Birds have evolved long slender bills where they need to poke into things to obtain food. An OYSTERCATCHER probes into mud for worms and even opens mussels and oyster shells to obtain the soft-bodied animal within. The slender beaks of hummingbirds and their extensible tongues are mainly for reaching inside flowers to obtain the sweet nectar. Spear-shaped bills are designed for catching fish and are found in HERONS and KINGFISHERS.

The scaly toes, feet and legs of birds are designed for walking, perching, grasping, snatching, climbing and fighting. Like beaks, there are many different shapes. Swimmers, such as penguins and ducks, have webs between the toes for pushing and steering through the water. Perching birds of the large order Passeriformes all have toes that can curl around a branch. Climbing birds, such as woodpeckers, have toes with strong, hook-like claws and usually two toes point forwards and two backwards to give better anchorage.

Birds of prey have powerful toes with strong piercing claws (or talons) which grasp the prey. Flightless birds show a reduction in the number of toes. A CASSOWARY has three while an OSTRICH has only two, although one is very large.

Above: This cassowary's head clearly shows its ear and part of its bony casque.

Below: The woodcock has eyes that can see through a complete 360°. This makes it less of a vulnerable target for predators as it busily probes the leaf-litter with its long, sensitive bill.

Senses

The most important senses of a bird are sight, then sound, with smell, touch and taste being not so well developed. The eyes of most birds are found on the sides of the head and are only slightly moveable in their sockets. Highly flexible necks enhance vision. When a bird such as a blackbird or robin cocks its head, it is not listening but bringing its eye into a position for better vision. An OWL can turn its head almost full circle.

It may come as a surprise to know that birds have ears, although the openings are usually hidden beneath a feathered head. There are no ear flaps, unlike in mammals, as these would impair flight. Their hearing is excellent and studies suggest their response to sounds is about ten times more rapid than that of humans. Experiments have shown that owls can catch prey, such as mice and voles, by sound alone, and plovers and lapwings can hear earthworms underground.

Smell is important to only a few birds. The

---

mammals or insects. They have even colonized European cities.
Kingfishers are thick-set birds with short necks and large bills. Many have crests, especially the American species. The majority of the 80 species are found in the tropics. Most have brilliant plumage, and often no more than a flash of colour is seen as they emerge from their waterside homes.
Kiwis are the smallest flightless birds and live only in New Zealand. They are quite rare and have an exceptional sense of smell.

L Lyrebirds are spectacular birds of east Australia. The male has a 30 cm long tail with lacy quills. He performs a shimmering courtship display in which his lacy plumes take on the shape of a lyre as they are spread over his back. Inhabiting forests and scrublands, these birds are shy and largely ground-dwelling.

M Macaws are some 18 species of large South American parrots. Most are very colourful and very noisy, feeding on seeds, nuts and fruit. The larger macaws can crack nuts with their strongly hooked beaks.
Mallee fowl of Australia are the best studied of Megapodes. These birds do not use their own body heat to hatch eggs. They live in the dry eucalyptus or 'mallee' scrub of southern Australia. They excavate a 1-metre-deep and 3-metre-wide hole, and fill it with vegetation and sand. The eggs are laid in early spring and rain starts the vegetation rotting. The parents regulate the heat build-up by altering the cover over the eggs. The male is thought to test the temperature with his tongue. The birds look like turkeys.

N Nightingales, although famous singers, are unimpressive, small russet-brown birds. They are shy inhabitants of woodlands.

Kingfisher

Nightingale

Birds

KIWI has a good sense of smell, the nostrils being placed at the tip of the upper bill and are used to find earthworms.

Migration and behaviour

Being able to fly allows birds to travel thousands of kilometres from summer breeding grounds to winter feeding grounds. How they navigate is still a mystery but the knowledge, on the whole, is inborn, and they are probably guided largely by the Sun, Moon, stars, and maybe even the Earth's magnetism.

Although a bird can easily cross water, and fly over mountains or deserts, a successful journey depends on the bird having sufficient energy in the form of food reserves for the strenuous flight. Some birds, such as ducks, geese, chaffinches and many songbirds, stop frequently for food. Birds try to avoid travelling over too wide an ocean or desert. For example, the white STORKS and other European migrants avoid crossing the widest

Above: Vast distances are covered annually by thousands of millions of migrating birds. They migrate in order to find adequate food supplies and optimum climatic conditions for survival. They seem to have instinctive navigational skills.

Below: Snow geese over South Dakota on their journey south from the Arctic tundra to California.

Nightjars are more often heard than seen, being nocturnal birds. During the day their remarkable speckled camouflage keeps them hidden on the forest floor.

Ospreys, known as the fish hawks in America, feed almost exclusively on fish. Their large toes have long, curved claws, and spiny scales under the toes hold the caught fish.

Ostriches, found south of the Sahara in Africa, are the largest living birds. Males stand 2·4 metres tall and weigh 130 kg. Flightless, they travel in groups of 10-50 birds, and are often found with antelopes and zebras.

Owls are largely nocturnal birds of prey. Over 130 species are recognized. Their short, very mobile necks enable them to turn their head almost 360°. Soft, fluffy plumage silences their flight, allowing them to catch prey unawares.

Oystercatchers are large, black and white, noisy birds, seen on coastal shores. The long, blunt, red bill is used to prise open oysters and mussels, kill small crabs and probe for worms.

P Parakeets are small parrots with long, pointed tails found mainly in the Indo-Malayan region. They eat grain and fruit, and travel in large flocks.

Passeriformes. This huge order contains all the perching birds or passerines (i.e. more than half the known species of birds). They all have four, similar, un-webbed toes. Their young are always naked and helpless on hatching.

Peafowl are often seen in zoos. The common peafowl originates from southern India and Sri Lanka. The male, or peacock, grows his magnificent long, eyed feathers to display to peahens. The peahen has a speckled brown plumage for camouflage on her ground nest.

Pelicans are instantly recognized by their large beak-pouch that holds two to three times as much food as its stomach, and is used as a scoop to catch fish.

Penguins are flightless, swimming birds of the coasts of the Southern Hemisphere. Their wings are paddle-like and non-folding for 'flying' through the water. They eat mainly fish, squid and crustaceans. Thick black and white plumage covers the whole body. The largest is the Emperor at

White pelican

Above: The cat display is a preliminary mating display of crested grebes. If both parties are interested, they then take part in the head-shaking ceremony.

Above: In the head-shaking ceremony, the 2 birds face each other with heads lowered threateningly. They then raise them and spread their head crests.

Above: The ghostly penguin display is where both birds dive and then rise up to face one another before sinking back into the water.

Above: The penguin dance follows head-shaking. They both dive to collect weeds. On the surface they sway from side to side paddling water.

Above: Ceremonies begin in mid-winter and continue for weeks and even months, thus keeping the pair together until nesting begins.

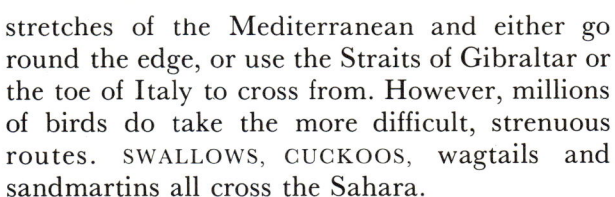

Above left: A courting peacock raises his 2-metre-high train high over his back in a shimmering fan studded with iridescent 'eye' markings.

Above right: A male frigate bird displays to a female by inflating his scarlet throat sac and vibrating his outstretched wings.

stretches of the Mediterranean and either go round the edge, or use the Straits of Gibraltar or the toe of Italy to cross from. However, millions of birds do take the more difficult, strenuous routes. SWALLOWS, CUCKOOS, wagtails and sandmartins all cross the Sahara.

One of the main ways birds express themselves is vocally. Songs, calls and sounds say what they think of their surroundings or animals that are close to them. Sounds vary from aggressive calls warning that a tom cat or bird of prey is approaching, to wonderful courtship songs that many birds perform in order to attract a female.

Birds compete for living space with other members of their own species. Robins, thrushes, and hummingbirds mark their landowner rights by song. A hummingbird flies continually around its small territory chasing away any rivals. Snipe make a drumming noise by vibrating their tail feathers as they plunge down over their territory.

A bird's plumage is also an important way of communicating. Colourful plumage, together with songs and dances, is an important way of attracting a mate. When a male robin sings, it puffs out its red chest to advertise its presence to a female. The BIRDS OF PARADISE are renowned for their colourful displays. As is often the case, it is the male who is the more brightly coloured, the female being a camouflaged mottled brown. This helps to hide her when she is incubating the eggs and caring for the young birds.

In some species of birds, such as penguins, grebes and herons, it is impossible to tell a male from a female. Yet the birds certainly perform wonderful courtship displays and establish a bond between a male and a female prior to nest building and breeding. Male frigate birds have expandable throat pouches which they inflate into huge red balloons to attract the female. Terns and kingfishers give presents of fish to their prospective partners, while courting GREBES give waterweeds to one another.

---

122 cm tall; the smallest is the blue penguin at 40 cm.

Puffins are members of the auk family. The large, parrot-like bills of both sexes grow a bright sheath during the breeding season. They nest in burrows which they dig with their feet. Fish are caught by diving.

R Rheas, sometimes called South American ostriches, are smaller than their African cousins, standing about 1·5 metres high. They are shy inhabitants of treeless open countryside where they live in flocks.

Robin

Robins are the small, plump, friendly birds of gardens and farmlands in Europe. The male sings a wistful and musical song to establish his breeding territory.

S Secretary birds are long-legged African hawks, so unlike other falcons and hawks that they are placed in a family of their own. They are so-named because of the long plumes on their head, which suggest a bunch of quill pens stuck behind a 'Dickensian' ear. They are well-known snake killers, but also kill small mammals and birds. They hunt mainly on foot.

Shrikes are small, bold, predatory perching birds. Essentially insect eaters, they will also catch small frogs, lizards, rodents and small

Shrike

birds as big as themselves. Their well-known habit of impaling their prey on thorns has earned them the name of 'butcherbirds'.

Sparrows are small, seed-eating birds. The house sparrow, native to Europe, western Asia and northern Africa is the most successful city and town dweller of all birds. In America, sparrows is the name given to various species of finches called buntings in Britain.

Starlings are jaunty birds with strong legs and feet. The 110 species are generally dark-coloured, most of them black with metallic sheens. Starlings are widely distributed and they mass in huge flocks.

Storks are long-necked,

Right: Swallows build open mud nests under the eaves of buildings.

Above: A grebe anchors its floating nest to reeds.

Above: A kingfisher pair excavate their nest-hole in a river bank.

Above: The South American oropendola's hanging nest is woven by the female from leaf fibres and vine stems.

Breeding and rearing

After territories and pairs have been formed, usually in the spring, then a couple can get down to the serious business of building a nest. A bird's nest will serve as a cradle for the eggs and as a temporary home for the young when they hatch. Usually, they will only leave when they can feed themselves and are able to fly. Nest shapes range from the simple cup-shaped nests of BLACKBIRDS to the intricate woven nests of WEAVER BIRDS. Some cliff-nesting birds like cormorants do not build any nest at all.

Birds use all kinds of material for their nest. Swallows use mud pellets. The TAILOR BIRD neatly 'sews' a large leaf together in its tropical Asian home and then makes its nest inside the leaf. Some cave swiftlets in Asia make their nests out of their saliva and it is these that are collected to make the delicacy, bird's nest soup. Male BOWERBIRDS make a courtship bower, often decorated with berries or brightly coloured flowers, where the female is courted and mated. She then goes off to build her nest nearby.

Many birds excavate burrows in the banks of streams or hillsides. These include kingfishers, bee-eaters and sand martins. Woodpeckers, hornbills, owls and parrots often prefer a hole in a tree trunk. The WOODPECKER can excavate a hole but the others rely on unoccupied holes.

The largest nest is built by the megapodes of Australia. A pair of birds construct a huge mound of rotting vegetation as much as three metres high and 16 metres across. The female lays her eggs in this mass and they are kept warm by the heat given off by the rotting vegetation. If the eggs become too hot the adults scratch away some vegetation to cool them off.

King and emperor PENGUINS lay single eggs which the males carry using their wide webbed feet. The egg is thus not touching the freezing ice and is kept warm by folds of feathered skin on the birds' bellies. The females go off to feed and

---

long-legged birds with broad wings and a long bill. They are usually coloured black and white. The majority of the 17 species fly with the neck outstretched and the feet trailing behind. The European white stork is regarded as a good omen.
Swallows are small, slender-bodied birds with very long pointed wings. Some of the 75 species have forked tails. Many species are migratory. Quick and extremely agile in the air, they are stranded if accidentally grounded because of their short limbs and wing width. They feed on insects caught in flight.

Swan and cygnets

Swans are graceful, large water birds related to geese and ducks. They are the largest of the waterfowl, their short legs being used mainly for propulsion. The long neck is used to reach below the surface of the water to obtain the waterweed on which they feed. The mute swan is not silent, as it can growl and hiss.
Swifts, the fastest fliers of all animals, rarely rest. They spend a lot of time on the wing with mouths agape to catch insects. Their small hooked feet enable them to cling to the sides of cliffs.

Tailor birds are ingenious 'weavers' of southeast Asia. They build their nests by sewing together the edges of one or two leaves with plant fibres or silk from insect cocoons. The cavity is lined with fine grasses, hairs and plant down.
Terns, found throughout the world, are members of the GULL family. Usually smaller and more graceful than gulls, they are often called sea swallows.
Thrushes are fine songsters that live everywhere except the polar regions. The bold mistle thrushes are the largest European species. The smaller, darker brown song thrushes are shyer although they have invaded some city gardens.
Tinamous are primitive, partridge-like birds of South America. They are poor fliers and do not migrate. An unusual fact is that the male incubates the eggs.
Toucans are birds of the South American jungles and have huge, brightly-coloured bills. The bill is hollow but well braced and serrated to help deal with its fruit diet. They are related to WOODPECKERS and barbets.

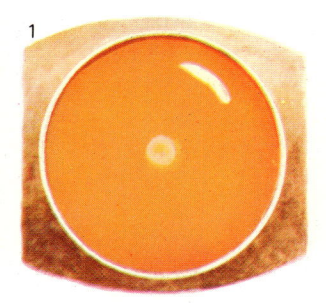

1 Above: Birth of a chick.
Incubation: The embryo in a new-laid hen's egg is visible as a pale spot on the yolk.

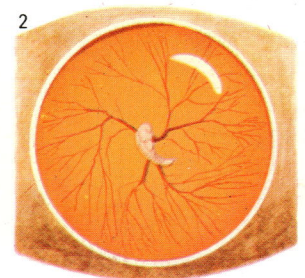

2 Day 5: The embryo is now surrounded by a network of blood vessels which bring nourishment from the yolk to the developing bird.

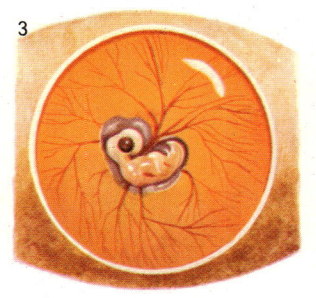

3 Day 12: The head has an eye and a beak, the limbs are beginning to form with the leg having 5 toes (one will disappear).

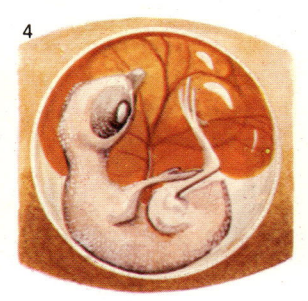

4 Day 18: The main flight feathers have developed and only 4 toes with claws are now present. The embryo is fully formed by day 24.

5 Day 29: The chick has grown rapidly during the last few days and chipped through the egg shell with its egg tooth and struggled free.

Golden plover

Blackbird

return just in time for hatching. The largest egg laid today is that of an OSTRICH which is about 1.5 kilograms. The smallest is the hummingbird's which weighs only 0.15 grams.

Each egg laid by a mated female bird contains a living, developing bird known as the embryo. It must be kept warm or it will die and so the parent birds, or just the female, sit on the eggs to keep them warm. The embryo develops, living on the yolk until it fills the inside of the egg and is ready to hatch. This development period is called incubation and its length varies considerably. Small singing birds hatch their eggs within a fortnight, while the royal albatross takes 81 days.

On hatching there are two main kinds of birds. There are those that are blind, naked and helpless, and there are those that at birth are fluffy chicks that can see and can leave the nest almost immediately.

Parents of fluffy, well-developed chicks usually lead them away from the nest on the day they

Above left: A young blackbird on hatching is blind and almost naked, and totally dependent on its parents for food and care. However, a golden plover chick is alert and covered with down, being able to leave the nest, run and find food for itself within 3 days.
Above right: A communal penguin crèche in Antarctica. Young penguins are 'in care' for 4 months or more, being looked after alternately by both parents and 'aunties' in the creches.

hatch. The nest is usually on the ground so although the chicks cannot fly, they will not come to harm. Ducks, grebes and geese lead their chicks to water and give them their first swimming lesson. Grebe chicks are often carried on the backs of their parents whilst swimming. Quails, grouse and pheasants take their young on hunting trips and hide them whilst the parents go off for food.

All chicks are fed, protected and guarded by their parents, or just by the female, until they have grown flight feathers and taken to the air. They are now fledglings. Many small singing birds fledge in under two weeks. The emperor penguin chick is fed by its parents for up to 39 weeks before it swims off, while a young wandering albatross may be looked after for up to 45 weeks. A king penguin chick has the longest parental attention. It is 'in care' for 10 to 13 months. Most birds will breed in the first season after they have hatched.

V Vultures play an important role in clearing up dead animals. The American vultures include the CONDOR, while the Afro-Asian vultures are related to hawks and eagles. They usually have a naked head and neck which enables them to keep reasonably clean when feeding on carcasses. They soar using hot air thermals.

W Warblers, are small insect-eating birds. Two distinct families are given this name. In the Old World the warblers are relatives of the thrushes, while in the Americas they are relatives of the tanagers. American warblers have brightly-coloured plumage and repetitive songs. The Old World species are rather dull in colour but have long and melodious songs.

Weaver birds of Eurasia and Africa are birds that have brought social development to its highest point in the bird kingdom. They are named after the highly complex communal nests many of them weave. These are elaborate suspended nests woven from vegetable fibres, some of which have entrance tunnels.

Woodpeckers are highly adapted for tree life, with gripping feet and stiff tails that act as props. Their straight, hard pointed, chisel-like bills dig into the tree bark and wood. A long, extensible tongue with a barbed tip extracts insects and grubs. Most species have loud harsh voices and also drum with their bill to advertise their presence.

Wrens are diminutive, busy, brown birds with big voices. They scurry around in the undergrowth searching for insects. The 59 species are wide ranging and have adapted to a variety of habitats.

Y Yellowhammers are small buntings with streaked yellow heads, commonly seen in open country. They are mainly seed eaters.

Vultures

The first land vertebrates were amphibians, part of their lives being spent in water. Their descendants, the reptiles, were the first true land animals, because they did not return to the water to breed.

Reptiles and Amphibians

Right: At almost 3 metres in length, the komodo dragon is the largest living lizard species. It kills and eats animals as big as hogs and small deer. A typical reptilian feature is its scaly skin which prevents the creature from drying out.

Above: When the mouth of an alligator or caiman, is closed, the 4th tooth in the lower jaw fits into a pit in the upper jaw and is hidden. In true crocodiles, the 4th tooth is still visible when the mouth is closed.

Amphibians were the first vertebrates to emerge from water onto the land, towards the end of the Devonian period. Even after some 350 million years they are still tied to their watery element, as most species, in order to breed, must enter water at certain times, and the young begin their development in water. Most adult amphibians have true lungs and can breathe air directly, but they also breathe through their moist skin and through the lining of the mouth which is well-supplied with blood vessels. Because of their moist skin, amphibians must always remain near or in water, or in places with high humidities, such as the steaming jungle. Only three groups of amphibians are found alive today: SALAMANDERS and NEWTS, often termed the Urodelans, the Caecilians, and the FROGS and TOADS which are often termed Anurans.

The reptiles that exist today evolved from amphibians but are a mere remnant of the forms that flourished some 200–70 million years ago during the age of the dinosaurs. One advantage over their amphibian relatives is that a reptile's body is protected from damage and dehydration by its covering of dry, horny scales. As a result reptiles are not tied to water, and can even live in hot deserts. Another advantage is that they do not have to return to the water to breed.

There are four orders of reptiles living today. The Chelonia include the sea TURTLES, land TORTOISES and freshwater TERRAPINS and are identified by their box-like bony shells. The largest reptiles and the closest surviving relations to the dinosaurs are the CROCODILES, GHARIALS,

Reference

A **Adders,** as they are known in Britain, are the common European VIPERS, although many other species exist. They are venomous, but the bite is rarely fatal to man. The females are longer than the males, being up to about 75 cm. They often have an X-shaped pattern on their head and a dark zigzag along the back.
Agama lizards, of which there are about 300 species, are the counterparts in

Adders

Europe, Asia, Africa and Australia of the South American IGUANAS.
Amphibians are the most primitive class of land-living vertebrates. In most cases, the young are tadpoles with gills for breathing in water. They change gradually into lung or skin breathing land-dwelling adults, although most still return to water for breeding. There are three living orders: the Apoda, Urodela and the Anura.
Anole lizards are some 165 species of IGUANAS living mainly in the Americas. Most species are between 13 and 23 cm long. Their expanded fingers and toes enable them to climb well.
Arrowpoison frogs are small, brightly-coloured frogs of the forests of Central and South America. All have potent poison glands and are so named because they are caught by the Indians and their poison is extracted to be used on arrow tips.
Axolotls are the larval stages of the American salamanders which breed while keeping their gilled larval form. This is known as neoteny and the species occur around Mexico City.

B **Bearded lizards** are Australian agamids which, when teased, turn bright yellow and orange. They soon regain their dark olive-brown colour. The beard consists of a great many pointed scales on the throat and neck which the lizard can greatly distend. This ferocious display, especially when its large mouth is opened, usually causes the enemy to hesitate and the lizard can escape.
Blind snakes are some 150 species that have adapted to burrowing and their eyesight ranges from poor to almost non-existent. Mainly tropical species, they feed on worms and millipedes.

Reptiles and Amphibians

Left: The basilisk of tropical America lives on river banks. Quite remarkably, it can rear up and run on its hind legs, using its tail as a balance. In this semi-erect posture it can actually run over the surface of water for short distances.

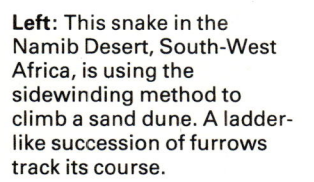

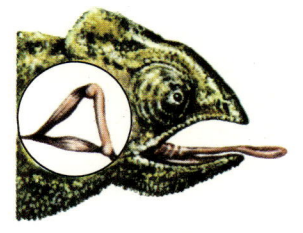

Left: This snake in the Namib Desert, South-West Africa, is using the sidewinding method to climb a sand dune. A ladder-like succession of furrows track its course.

Right: The chameleon is the sharp-shooter of the reptile world. Its sticky tongue is catapulted out when an insect flies too close.

alligators and CAIMANS of the order Crocodilia. The order Rhynchocephalia contains only one species, the TUATARA from New Zealand. The Squamata contains the LIZARDS and SNAKES which together make up the largest number of modern reptiles, as well as being the youngest group.

Feeding and movement

Most amphibians and reptiles are hunters, and swallow their prey whole. This explains why they have wide gapes to their mouths. They do not usually chew their food so no cheeks are needed. Amphibians feed mainly on invertebrates such as worms, insects and their larvae. Frogs and toads swim in water using their webbed hind feet to give most of the propulsion. On land they hop using their powerful back legs. Newts and salamanders swim by undulating their long body and tail, or walk and scurry on land with a twisted gait. The tongue in frogs and toads is fixed at the front end while the back end lies free. When an insect comes within range, the tongue is flicked out at high speed and the sticky end collects the prey and returns it to the mouth. Newts and salamanders do not have this type of tongue and so snap at their prey.

In the reptile group, many of the Chelonia, all of which lack teeth, are vegetarians. The carnivorous reptiles, such as snakes and lizards, seize prey by their teeth. The salivary glands in the mouth coat the prey so it is slippery and it can then be swallowed and taken into the digestive system more easily. Chameleons catapult their muscular tongue out to capture small prey.

Snakes move by one of four different methods, or a combination of all four. Wriggling their bodies in S-shaped waves that pass from the head down the length of the body is the most common method. This type of movement relies on the snake's body touching stones, pebbles or plants in its path to push itself forwards. The 'concertina' method is where the snake loops its body

Below: A snake has independently moveable jawbones that allow quite sizeable animals to pass down into its elastic throat.

Boa constrictors live in the dry forests and scrub of South America. Their patterned body blends in with their surroundings. They kill their rodent prey by constriction. They can grow up to 6 metres long.

Boomslangs are green African savanna snakes that grow up to 2 metres long. They are one of very few colubrid snakes whose bite can be fatal to man.

Bullfrogs are large frogs with very deep voices, which when heard quite close sound like a bull's roar. The American bullfrog is the largest North American frog at 20 cm, and lives up to 16 years.

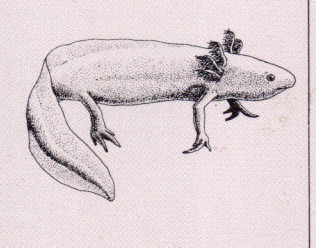

C **Caecilians** are some 160 species of legless amphibians living in South America, tropical Africa, the Seychelles and south-east Asia. They look like earthworms because their grooved skin makes them look segmented.

Caimans are closely related to alligators but differ from them in that the bony plates of the skin continue round from the armour-plated back to the underside of these animals. They are found in Central and South America.

Chameleons are some 85 species of tree-dwelling lizards, mainly from Africa and Madagascar. Their feet are adapted for grasping by having 2 toes opposed to the other 3, and their tails are prehensile. Their eyes move independently and the sticky extensible tongue shoots out to catch insects.

Chelonia. This reptile order contains the TURTLES, TORTOISES and TERRAPINS. The basic design of the 250 species has hardly changed over the last 200 million years. All the species possess a shell of bony plates covered by horny scales which form an upper shell, the carapace, and an under shell, the plastron.

Axolotl

Cobra

Reptiles and Amphibians

Left: A gecko has cling pads on its feet that catch on any tiny surface irregularities – even glass can be scaled.
Right: Jacobson's organ is the specialized sensor that enables snakes to track prey.
Below: This Texas indigo snake is about to slough its skin. Its flicking tongue picks up particles for analysis by Jacobson's organ.

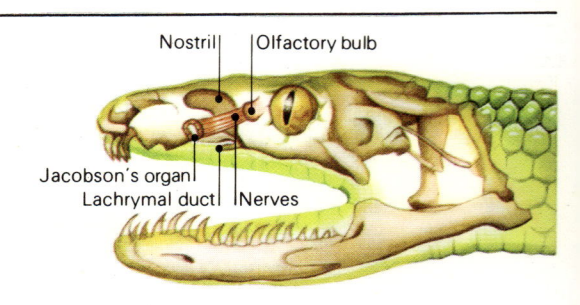

forwards, the 'rectilinear' method is similar to an earthworm's movement, and 'sidewinding' is used mainly in deserts and sandy places where the snake moves in a series of sideways steps across the surface of the dune.

As a snake moves along it continually flicks out its forked tongue to collect tiny particles from the air and ground. Sensitive cells in the Jacobson's organ in the roof of the mouth detect smells. The reptile can thus track down prey. To overpower its prey a snake uses one of two methods. One method is on having caught the prey with its teeth, the snake then winds its body around until its victim can no longer breathe. These constrictors include the BOAS and PYTHONS. Other snakes use poison to overcome their victims. Snake venom usually acts upon the blood and tissues, or upon the nervous system. SEA SNAKES, COBRAS, VIPERS and PIT-VIPERS all have poison glands which are modified salivary glands in the upper jaw. In the upper front row of the teeth are two or more big poison fangs that are visible when the jaws are open. On biting the prey, the fangs work like hypodermic syringes. The poison runs through the tubes inside the hollow teeth and is injected into the prey. Prey larger than the snake itself can still be swallowed as the jaws are loosely hinged and the whole region of the mouth, neck and ribs is very elastic, so although swallowing takes quite some time, it is eventually achieved.

Below: The elongated snout of this Indian gavial is associated with its almost exclusive diet of fish, caught by a sideways sweep.

All crocodiles have long snouts and tremendous jaws which have peg-like teeth in them. On land they are often seen lazing in the sun. In the water they are almost completely submerged except for the eyes and nostrils and the leathery back breaking the water's surface. When it is close enough to a victim the crocodile moves with a sudden burst of energy, grasps the victim in its jaws or knocks it over with its lashing tail. A large animal such as an antelope or deer is then dragged underwater to drown. The air-breathing channel in the crocodile is completely separated from its mouth so that the reptile can hold and tear and swallow food underwater, yet breathe at the same time.

Cobras are highly poisonous snakes related to mambas, coral snakes and SEA SNAKES. Their short tubular, or grooved, fangs inject poison as the snake chews its victim. The king cobra, or hamadryad, of south-east Asia is one of the largest poisonous snakes and can be up to 5 metres long.

Constrictors are some 76 species of large, non-poisonous snakes that kill their prey by constricting. The victim is encoiled and squeezed until it can no longer breathe and dies of suffocation. Nearly all the species are tropical, the largest one being the reticulated PYTHON which can measure up to 10 metres.

Crocodiles live mainly in tropical rivers although the estuarine crocodiles do venture out to sea. They are known to attack man but mainly prey on large animals such as cattle. CAIMANS and alligators are included in the same family.

E **Edible frogs** are bright green with yellowish thighs and a dorsal stripe. They are found in Europe and the back legs have been a favourite item of food since Roman and probably prehistoric times.

F **Frilled lizards** of Australia and New Guinea can run on their hind legs with the tail and forelegs off the ground. They confront their enemies by raising their frill and opening their mouth which makes them look much larger.

Frogs are generally smooth, slimy, shiny-skinned AMPHIBIANS with very long hind legs that enable them to make very long hops. Their TOAD relatives usually have dry, rough skins with wart-like growths on them. They have shorter back legs and do not make such long hops. The two names are often interchanged.

Fangs of a puff adder

G **Geckos** are some 300 species of lizards that are found in tropical and sub-tropical regions. The species best known to man is the house gecko which can be seen, usually after dark, running across walls and over ceilings in search of food. They can do this as they have special plates on the under-surface of their toes called lamellae which have adhesive powers. All geckos make soft chirruping or clucking sounds. Tokay geckos have very loud cries.

Gharials are long, thin-snouted crocodiles that live

Reptiles and Amphibians

Right: The female green turtle of tropical waters lays up to 100 eggs in a pit dug in the sand above the high water tidemark. After laying she struggles back to the sea. On hatching, the young turtles instinctively head for the sea but predators such as gulls and crabs take a very high number for food.

Above: On laying her eggs, a female carpet python pushes them together into a heap and coils herself around them until they hatch. This may take up to 80 days.

Reptile reproduction

Most reptiles lay soft, leathery eggs. A few give birth to live young, such as the common lizard and CHAMELEON. The developing embryo inside the protective egg case is supplied with a large yolk to nourish it, and a special sac, the allantois, enables oxygen and carbon dioxide to pass between the young and the outside world. The young reptiles, whether alligator, snake or turtle, look like miniature adults and do not have the larval stages of the amphibians.

The sexes look alike in all groups except in certain lizard species. Male agamas and iguanas become brightly coloured and territorial during the breeding season.

Mating is preceded by some kind of courtship in most reptiles. A male giant tortoise acknowledges the approach of a female by nodding his head, and he makes low pitched roars before mating. Bull alligators roar in the courting season and this is probably done to attract females to them. Male Galapagos IGUANAS and MONITOR LIZARDS have ritual combats between one another. Male RATTLESNAKES, vipers and mambas all entwine their bodies and rear up and push against one another until one glides away exhausted. In some instances a female has been seen resting nearby and has been courted by the victorious male, having overcome his rival and put him to flight.

Eggs are usually deposited in holes dug in the ground. The female turtle lays her eggs in a dry, warm hole in the sand of a tropical beach above the high tide mark. Crocodiles and some alligators are known to build nests and the batch of 20-80 eggs are carefully guarded. The female sits on the nest or lurks nearby. When the young are trying to hatch, the female has been seen to remove the vegetation to help the young escape.

Stories, such as Rudyard Kipling's *Rikki-Tikki-Tavi*, of cobras guarding their eggs are not entirely fictitious. Indian cobras and pythons brood the eggs by coiling round them.

Amphibian reproduction

Most amphibians have to return to freshwater to breed. Their eggs are usually fertilized outside the body. In frogs and toads, the male clings to the female's back, and sprays his semen over the eggs as they emerge from the female. They are laid in huge numbers in jelly-like strings or clumps in most species.

Some frogs take great care of their brood. The male midwife toad carries the eggs around until hatching, wrapped round his hind legs. He spreads the eggs out just as they are about to hatch. The marsupial frog of Brazil keeps the eggs safe in a pocket of skin.

---

in the Indus, Ganges and Brahmaputra rivers in India. This snout is an adaptation for catching fish.

Giant tortoises are 2 huge, long-lived species, one inhabiting the Seychelles and Aldabras, and the other inhabiting the Galapagos Islands. They probably reached these islands via ocean currents, being able to withstand long periods of starvation. They are strictly herbivorous.

Gila monsters, the only venomous lizards, are black and yellow beaded in appearance and live in south-west North America and Mexico. The poison glands are in the lower jaws.

Greater crested newts are Eurasian AMPHIBIANS. The females are larger than the males, growing up to 18 cm long. Males have a dorsal crest which is absent in the females.

Giant tortoise

Green turtles are found living in all warm seas, but mainly within the tropics where they are killed to make into genuine turtle soup. This, and the egg-collecting done by man, has led to the species becoming quite rare in places. Certain beaches are now protected for breeding purposes.

Horned vipers are also known as sand vipers. The broad head has the tip of its nose drawn out to form an erect and scaly horn. They live in North Africa, Arabia and south-west Asia.

Iguanas are some 700 species of lizards found mainly in tropical America. They usually live in trees, but are strong swimmers

Iguana

Reptiles and Amphibians

Right: Most frogs mate and lay their eggs (spawn) in water. Jelly surrounds each egg and acts as protection **(1)**. At first the tadpole breathes through feathery gills, but these are lost when internal lungs develop. **(2)**. By 10 weeks the tadpole is frog-like **(3)** and within a month the tiny amphibian can leave the water **(4)**.

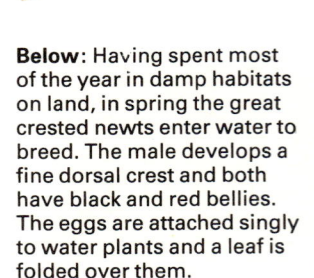

In newts and salamanders, the eggs are fertilized within the body of the female and before pairing there is usually an elaborate courtship display. The males often develop bright mating colours and after an aquatic courtship dance, he deposits his packet of sperms, known as a spermatophore, beside the female. She picks it up and stores the sperm until it is needed to fertilize her eggs.

Below: Having spent most of the year in damp habitats on land, in spring the great crested newts enter water to breed. The male develops a fine dorsal crest and both have black and red bellies. The eggs are attached singly to water plants and a leaf is folded over them.

Most amphibian young go through various larval stages. On hatching they are limbless and have external feathery gills and a broad tail. As they develop, legs appear, the external gills are lost when the lungs begin to function and the tadpole begins to resemble a small adult. The tail fin in Anurans is re-absorbed and the small adult is complete and can leave the water, only returning to breed.

and take readily to water. The marine iguana of the Galapagos is the only lizard to live in the sea.

Lizards come in all shapes and sizes from a few centimetres to the 3-metre-long Komodo dragon. The slow-worms and burrowing lizards have lost their limbs and have small eyes and ears. A few lizards, such as the skinks, give birth to live young, but most lay eggs. Many lizards, such as the CHAMELEONS, can change their skin colour to match their surroundings.

Monitor lizards are large, fast-running predators that live throughout the warmer regions of Africa and Australasia. Among the 24 species are the 3-metre-long Komodo dragon and the Nile monitor. The Komodo dragon will eat domesticated animals while most monitors eat amphibians, birds, and eggs.

Newts are a type of SALAMANDER and the 20 species belong to the genus *Triturus*. Most species are found in Europe. They have short legs, a long body and tail, and a typically moist skin. They are mainly land-dwelling but return to water for the breeding season. During this season, the male develops a crest.

Pythons belong to the BOA CONSTRICTOR family and are found mainly in Africa, Asia and Australasia. The reticulated python can reach a length of over 10 metres. The royal, diamond, and Indian pythons, are amongst the most beautifully patterned snakes.

Pit vipers are so-called because they have a pit in the side of the face between the eye and the nostril that acts as a sense organ. Rattlesnakes, bush-masters and fer-de-lances are all pit vipers.

Rattlesnakes are so-called because their tails end in a series of horny, interlocking segments. When the tail is vibrated

Eastern diamondback rattlesnake

Reptiles and Amphibians

Reptile behaviour

Like fish and amphibians, reptiles are often said to be 'cold-blooded'. As a result they exhibit a common act of behaviour, that of basking in the sun to raise their body temperature. Their body temperature varies with their surroundings. In very cold climates they become lethargic and grass snakes, common lizards and pet tortoises must hibernate through the cold winter months. Reptiles flourish best in tropical conditions where they can be active enough to compete with other creatures.

The wear and tear to the skin of lizards and snakes means that it needs to be replaced at intervals. There are several moulting periods each year. In most lizards, such as the chameleon, the skin is shed in large flakes, while in most snakes it is shed in a single continuous slough. It is possible to tell when a snake is about to moult as the eyes take on a bluish tinge. A snake's eye is covered by fused transparent eyelids and these are replaced in the moult.

Some reptiles have the striking ability to change the colour of their skin. CHAMELEONS are the most accomplished at this and lighting conditions seem to be the most important factor influencing colour change. In complete darkness the animal becomes very pale, and it tends to darken when exposed to light.

Many reptiles have appendages growing from their bodies. There are horned chameleons, and IGUANAS and AGAMA LIZARDS have throat fans. The large frill of the frilled lizard and the spiny 'beard' of the bearded lizard can be raised and lowered rapidly and displayed in aggressive or courtship gestures.

One of the most interesting skin structures is the rattlesnake's rattle. It consists of a number of interlocking horny segments. It is now generally accepted that the rattle warns intruders to keep their distance, although previous theories ranged from a mating to a distress call.

Above: A chameleon sheds its skin in quite large irregular plates, unlike the single continuous slough in snakes.
Above right: A hog-nosed snake lies inert, belly uppermost and tongue protruding, feigning death. It will come to 'life' when all is clear.
Below: An Australian frilled lizard's warning device is to erect its frill and face its aggressor. This makes it look much larger.

---

rapidly, it produces a dull hissing sound (rattle) to warn enemies. A new segment is added each time the skin is shed but the end ones continually break off, so 6 to 10 segments is usual.

S **Salamander** is the name applied to many species of families of the order Urodela. The spotted, or common, European salamander lives in hilly districts and hides by day under stones or decaying leaves. It is black with bright yellow spots. The secretions of its skin are poisonous to small animals. The AXOLOTL of Mexico is a salamander. The giant salamander of Japan is the largest known and can grow to a length of about a metre. Its flesh can be eaten.
Sea snakes have successfully adapted to a marine life. Most species have flattened bodies for swimming and give birth to live young. They produce an extremely potent venom.
Skinks are some 700 species of LIZARD that have small limbs, although some are limbless. Half the species lay eggs while the rest give birth to live young.

Snakes are reptiles that are legless, shed their skin completely, have no external ear openings and usually swallow their prey whole. There are about 2800 species. They kill by either injecting their prey with venom or by constriction.

T **Terrapins** are freshwater TORTOISES or TURTLES. Americans call large water turtles, terrapins, while the British sometimes call them water tortoises. They are termed cooters or sliders in the southern United States.
Toads are strictly members of the family Bufonidae. They are more slow moving than FROGS, their heads are more rounded and their skins are warty. Toads lay their eggs in strings as opposed to the cluster-type spawn laid by frogs.

Toads mating

Amphibian behaviour

Amphibians have few defences against their enemies and so most of them rely on protective coloration to camouflage themselves. Most frogs and toads are brown, yellow or green to match their habitat. Tree frogs are usually as green as the leaves on which they live, and so are very difficult to see. Being so well camouflaged, and also quite small, means that at the breeding season sound is very important in getting the sexes together.

A powerful weapon of defence is poison and many amphibians are equipped with poison glands in their skin. In most toads the poison glands are massed into warty lumps so that a predator on picking up a toad in its jaws will quickly drop it. The arrowpoison tree frogs of South America are so deadly poisonous that they advertise their danger to enemies by being vivid reds and blacks or yellow and blacks. These frogs are the source of supply of the poison kurari to the local Indian tribes for use on the arrow tips in their blowpipes.

The AXOLOTL of Mexican freshwater pools is the Peter Pan of the amphibian world. It never grows up. The aquatic larval forms retain their gills and yet reach sexual maturity. They then breed without metamorphosing into adult salamanders. This is due to a lack of iodine in the thyroid gland which triggers off the life cycle changes.

Below: On land, the strong hind legs of a frog are used for jumping. The impact on landing is taken by the short front limbs.

Above: A Costa Rican flying frog caught 'in flight'.

Below: A painted reed frog utters a mating call by inflating its throat pouch.

Tortoises are members of the reptilian family Testudiinidae. Their feet have adapted to a life on land. In most species the carapace (shell) is highly domed.

Tree frogs, of which there are some 600 species, are amphibians adapted for a life in trees. They can hang by one toe from a twig, balance on a swaying stalk or press themselves flat, vertically on a tree trunk. They can do all this because the tips of their toes and fingers have suction pads.

Tuatara is the primitive, lizard-like reptile of the order Rhynchocephalia. It has teeth that are fused to the edges of the jaws, and a third eye on top of its head. Although once widespread in New Zealand, it now survives under protection only in the Bay of Plenty.

Turtle is the name given to the marine species that are oceanic, and the mud (or soft-shelled) species which live only in freshwater. Marine turtles have broad, paddle-shaped limbs and include the GREEN TURTLE, the hawksbill, loggerhead and leathery turtles. Most species are endangered due to man hunting them and taking their eggs.

V Vipers are distinguished from other poisonous snakes by the fact that their fangs are attached to a moveable bone, the maxillary. When not in use the fangs lie backwards in the mouth in a horizontal position. The family Viperidae contains the true vipers and the PIT VIPERS. The bite of larger species, such as the gaboon viper and puff adder, is usually fatal to man. Smaller vipers, such as the European viper or ADDER, cause pain and swelling but rarely death to man.

Orsini's viper

Fishes were the first animals with backbones. Most fishes live in Sun-warmed surface waters, but some have adapted to icy polar waters and others exist in ocean trenches some 11 kilometres deep.

Fishes

Fishes evolved from invertebrate ancestors over 440 million years ago. They were the first group to have a backbone giving support to the body. The various fins projecting from the body are supported by parts of the skeleton. Fishes are aquatic cold-blooded vertebrates, virtually all of which breathe by gills. In the vast oceans and waters which cover about 75 per cent of our world, there are over 20,000 species of fish. They exploit every available habitat and show a great variety in size, shape, colour and behaviour.

The majority of fishes are bony fish of the class Osteichthyes, but there are some 600 species of cartilaginous fish of the class Chondrichthyes, which includes the SHARKS and RAYS. The most primitive fishes are the 50 or so species of jawless LAMPREYS and HAGFISHES of the class Agnatha.

The bodies of most fishes are covered with scales, which vary from the teeth-like scales of sharks to the plate-like scales of herrings and salmon. In the bony fishes the scales can be used to find out the age of the fish. Under a microscope a scale is seen to be made up of rings, each ring representing a year's growth. This is similar to the growth rings in tree trunks. In other fishes, such as the SEAHORSES and armoured CATFISHES, nearly all the body is covered in a protective bony armour. Some fishes have protective spines instead of scales.

Most fishes have two kinds of fins, paired and unpaired. The paired fins are the pectorals and the pelvics, one of each is on either side of the body. The unpaired fins are the dorsals on the back and the ventrals and anals on the underside. The tail (or caudal) fin in most fishes is the main means of propulsion.

How fishes swim

There is a great variation in the shape, size and use of the fins depending on where the fish lives and how it moves. The pectoral fins are usually

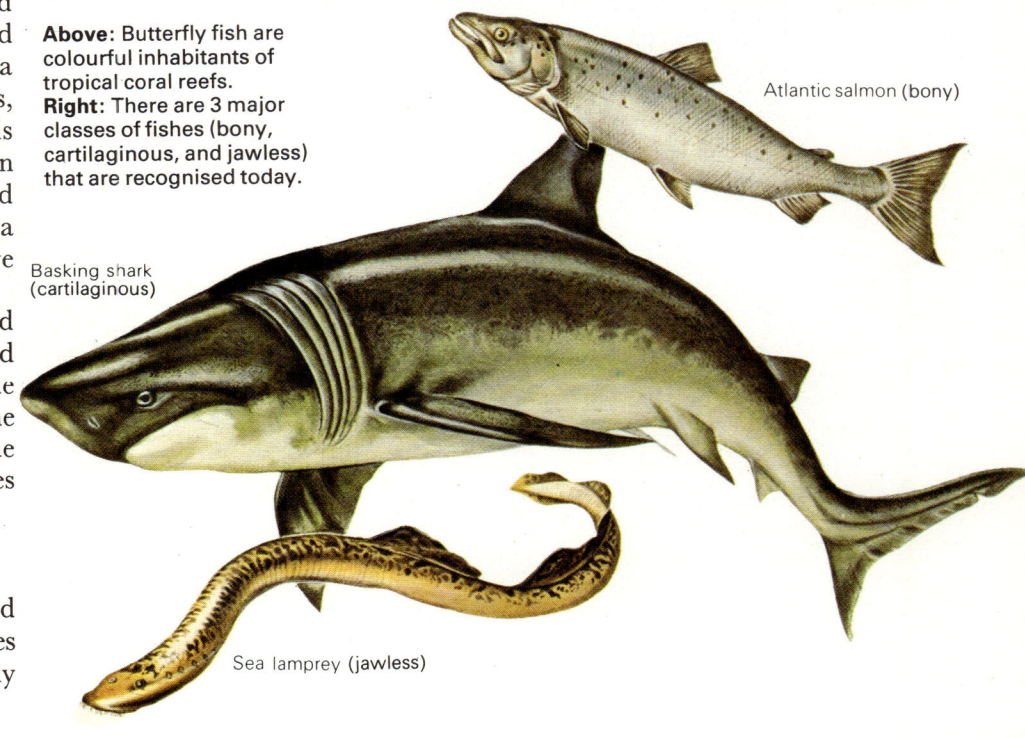

Above: Butterfly fish are colourful inhabitants of tropical coral reefs.
Right: There are 3 major classes of fishes (bony, cartilaginous, and jawless) that are recognised today.

Atlantic salmon (bony)

Basking shark (cartilaginous)

Sea lamprey (jawless)

Reference

A **Angel fishes** are small fishes that have laterally compressed bodies. They are among the most beautiful fishes in the world and inhabit both freshwater (CICHLIDS) and tropical coral reefs. They show a fantastic range of colours and patterns in the 150 species. Some are up to 60 cm long. The related BUTTERFLY FISHES are usually much smaller.
Angler fishes have a moveable 'fishing rod' fixed to their upper jaw that acts like a lure. The 'rod' is a modified spine of the dorsal fin. When a small fish is attracted to the lure, the angler gulps it into its mouth at a terrific speed.
Archer fishes can shoot a powerful jet of water at an unsuspecting insect lying up to a metre away. The victim drops into the water and is gulped down. They live in south-east Asia and Australasia.

B **Barracudas** are streamlined, fast-moving, carnivorous fish. Divers sometimes fear an attack by these 2-metre-long giants more than sharks.

Veil-tail angelfish

Butterfly fishes are colourful, tropical reef fishes closely related to ANGEL FISHES. Their small mouths and extended snouts are adapted for picking up invertebrates from cracks and crevices in coral. There are also unrelated freshwater species.

C **Carp** are large relatives of the GOLDFISH found in most temperate freshwater habitats. They can weigh over 25 kg. They have 4 barbels, 2 at each side of the mouth. Golden carp, bred by the Japanese, are spectacular fish for garden pools.

Catfishes are usually found in African, Asian and South American waters, although others live farther north. Most species have barbels to help find their food. They are either scale-less or are covered with bony protective plates (armoured catfishes).

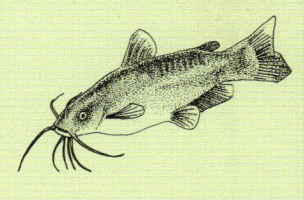

Catfish

used for steering, or for slow movements as in seahorses. In the rays, the pectorals are huge and are practically the only means of locomotion. The fins are slowly flapped up and down and waves travel down the huge muscular fins to propel the animal along. The pelvic fins assist in keeping a fish steady. In the so-called FLYING FISHES, the pectorals are very long and almost reach the tail. When the fish has got up enough speed to shoot out of the water, these fins are expanded and the fish glides above the waves, the fins acting merely as aerofoils.

The majority of fishes that swim quickly use body movements and the tail fin. The body movements are caused by alternately contracting and relaxing body muscles known as myomeres. This causes the fish to wiggle from side to side in an S-shape. Water is pushed aside by the forward motion of the fish's head. It moves first to the left, then the right, the muscles contracting alternately down the fish's body to drive the fish forward. The sailfish is reckoned to be the fastest fish.

How fishes feed

Movement is important to fishes, firstly to escape being eaten by bigger fishes and other marine creatures, and also in finding food to eat. A large number of bony fishes are fish-eaters (piscivorous), such as the COD, PERCH, BASS and PIKE, and they usually have strong pointed teeth with which to seize their prey. The pike's large mouth simply bristles with teeth, not only in the jaws, but also on the roof of the mouth and the tongue. The pike lurks in a clump of vegetation and as soon as a victim, usually a fish, comes within reach it is snapped up. Hungry pike will even eat their own kind. They are the true cannibals of their world.

Another fish renowned for its ferocity is the PIRANHA of the rivers of South America. They live in groups and have sharp powerful jaws equipped with sharp cutting teeth. Although their usual diet is smaller fishes, they will attack any animal unlucky enough to fall in the water. It is then cut to pieces in a very short time.

Below: To swim forwards, most fishes move their body from side to side by the alternate expansion and contraction of body muscles, the myomeres. The various fins aid movement also. The illustration of a shark swimming shows how the body is curved and how the flexure moves backwards from the head to the tail.

Right: The sand tiger shark shows his rows of sharp, pointed teeth.

Below: Rays, such as this Manta ray swimming over the Great Barrier Reef, swim by flapping their greatly enlarged pectoral fins.

Chimaeras are strange-looking relatives of SHARKS and RAYS. The upper jaw is fixed to the skull and the male has a clasper in front of his eyes that probably has some courtship function. In some species, the long dorsal spine carries a sting.
Cichlids are an aggressive family of some 600 species found in tropical freshwaters of the world, but mainly in South America. Many species are very popular with aquarium owners, especially angel fish, the pompadour fish and the MOUTHBROODERS.

Chimaera monstrosa

Codfishes occur chiefly in the northern seas and are, with the haddock, pollack and whiting, some of the world's most valuable food fishes. Most species live near the sea bottom and so are trawled by fishermen. The Atlantic cod is the largest of the 150 species in its family (Gadidae). It has a small whiskery barbel under the chin.
Coelacanths are living fossil fishes. They were thought to have become extinct some 65 million years ago until 1 was trawled up off East London, South Africa in 1938. The leg-like fins can move in all directions and are probably used to stir up mud on the sea floor when searching for prey.

D Dogfishes are small SHARKS. In Europe they are fished commercially. The common dogfish is an inshore, shallow-water species.

E Eels, of which there are over 300 species, are mainly marine and live in shallow water. The majority are scale-less and the dorsal and anal fins are continuous with the tail fin. Most eels

Eels

Fishes 35

Sharks are the other notable flesh-eaters and these cartilaginous fishes have several rows of teeth in their jaws. As they are worn down at the front of the jaw they are replaced from behind. The teeth of the great white shark, or man-eater, are the most formidable and powerful of all sharks. The white shark feeds mainly on fishes, but porpoises, water birds and even sealions are taken, as well as humans.

Many fishes feed on small aquatic insects and their larvae. TROUT will leap out of the water to catch flies and gnats near the surface. The ARCHER FISH are so-called because of the fact they 'shoot down' insects with jets of water.

Fishes breathe through gills and these are always found between the mouth and the beginning of the food tract or gut. This region is called the pharynx. In sharks, the walls of the pharynx have several narrow gill slits which open to the outside. Water is taken in through the mouth and passed over the gills and out again. In bony fishes, the gill slits have a moveable cover

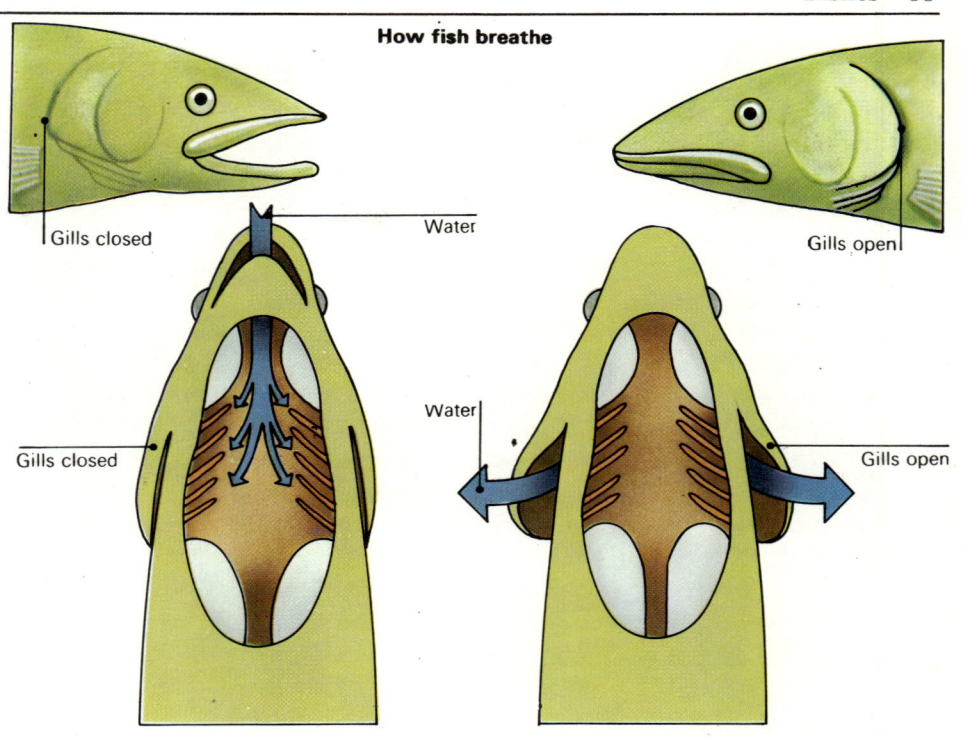

How fish breathe

Below: The archer fish of south-east Asia gets its name from its curious feeding method. On seeing a fly or insect over its watery home, the fish takes aim and squirts a drop or two of water from its mouth at its victim. An adult fish can eject a jet of water over a distance of 90 cm.

Above: When the mouth of a fish opens, oxygenated water is drawn in. The fish extracts the oxygen and the water is then passed out through the gills.

Below: The piranha of South American rivers swim together in schools. They can grow up to 38 cm long. Their jaws are armed with sharp cutting teeth that can quickly slice up the flesh of other fish or mammals.

---

have a transparent, ribbon-like larva known as a leptocephalus. It eventually changes into a small eel.
Electric eels are freshwater South American fishes of the family Electrophoridae, not closely related to true EELS. They have electric organs which enable them to establish electrical fields around their bodies as an aid to locating enemies and stunning prey. The anal fin helps the fish to move.

F **Fighting fishes** from Thailand are bred and used for sport. The wild ancestor is small and dull compared to aquarium breeds. Varieties in captivity range from cream-coloured with red fins to a purplish-blue. Only the males are aggressive, especially during the breeding season. The male builds a bubble nest for the eggs, and then he guards the nest and young.
Flatfishes are several species that change (undergo skeletal metamorphosis) from being normal larval fish with eyes on each side of the head to a flatfish that lives on the bottom of the

Plaice

sea and spends the rest of its adult life there. The eye on the underside migrates to the opposite side of the head and the mouth becomes twisted. The blind side does not develop pigment but the upper side is able to vary its colour pattern with the surroundings. Many flatfishes are valuable food fishes, such as the flounder, plaice, turbot, sole and halibut.
Flying fishes are small, slender, bony fishes that are found in the surface waters of the oceans. Large pectoral fins enable them to glide through the air. Some species cover over 150 metres in one flight.

G **Goldfishes** in the wild are plain, brownish CARP-like creatures. Today, many different types of domestic goldfish have been bred, mainly pioneered by the Japanese.

called the operculum. The gills are supported by a special part of the skeleton called the gill arches. As water is passed over the gills, oxygen passes through the thin walls of the gills into the bloodstream, and the waste carbon dioxide passes from the blood through the gills and into the water.

Fishes that breathe air

Most fishes when taken out of water die because their gills cannot function properly. Although air contains more oxygen than water, the gills cannot extract it, and so the fish suffocate. There are fishes, however, that can breathe by other methods. EELS often make considerable journeys over wet ground. This is because they are able to breathe through their skin as long as it is kept moist, just like frogs and newts.

Climbing perch, FIGHTING FISH and certain catfishes of Africa and Asia have accessory breathing organs off the gill chambers. The LUNGFISHES, as their name suggests, have lungs and they can breathe air. The lung is an outgrowth of the gullet and has evolved from the swim bladder, whose function in most fishes is to give buoyancy. The ability to breathe air allows lungfishes to survive periods of drought in Africa, Australia and South America.

Above: An African lungfish can lie dormant for weeks or months in its mud cocoon for the duration of the dry season. It has a tiny breathing hole to the surface.
Below left: After spending years at sea maturing and feeding, salmon navigate their way back to their freshwater birthplace possibly by the Sun and a sense of smell.
Below right: A cleaner fish here provides a 'doctoring' service to a coral cod by eating bacteria, fish lice and fungus from its skin and inside its mouth.

Behaviour and breeding in fishes

In adapting to various habitats some strange aquatic partnerships occur, for instance between Damselfishes and tropical sea anemones in the Pacific Ocean. Even more extraordinary are the barber (or cleaner) fish who clean external parasites from the skins and gills of other fish. These fishes are usually brightly coloured as if to advertise their presence to 'customers'. They certainly help to maintain the well-being of other fishes and are especially abundant in tropical regions. Some fishes, such as FLATFISHES, can change colour to match their backgrounds.

Fish migration is associated with the reproductive cycle of the species and with the availability of food. Commercially exploited fishes, such as the blue-fin tuna (tunny) and the Atlantic SALMON have been well studied. The migration of salmon is complex, the fish leaving their birthplace in the headstreams of freshwater rivers to spend several years at sea feeding and maturing. They then return to the river of their birth to spawn. Experiments have shown they have an excellent sense of direction and their acute sense of smell enables them to detect their original birthplace. The European and American eels are famous for their migrations from freshwaters to the Sargasso Sea, the young then

H Hagfishes are jawless fish that remain buried in mud, gravel or sand by day. At night they emerge to scavenge on dead animals or any waste organic material. Some are parasites on living fishes. They have lost their eyes and hunt for food by touch and smell.

Goldfish

Herrings are silvery fish that travel in huge shoals and are very important food fishes. They make unpredictable seasonal migrations and move into shallow waters for spawning.

L Lampreys attach themselves by suckers to the sides of fishes. They rasp through the skin and flesh and drain the victim of blood. The adults usually die after they have reproduced.

Lantern fishes are small, deep-sea fishes that have light-producing organs, or photophores, along their sides. They migrate daily from 1,000 metres or more to feed near the surface.

Lungfishes are air breathing relics from the DEVONIAN PERIOD (*see page* 4). African and South American lungfishes have eel-shaped bodies. They have 2 lungs and aestivate (hibernate) in dried mud with a breathing hole through periods of drought. The Australian species has only a single lung and dies quickly if its surroundings dry up.

M Man-eating shark is the term given to those SHARKS that are known to attack man. It is most often used to mean the great white SHARK, but others include the mako, tiger, sand, and hammerhead.

Mouthbrooders are species of CICHLIDS that brood their eggs inside the mouth. It is usually the male that does this. Even after hatching the young are held in the mouth for a short time. The young fish are thus guarded and whenever they stray too far or danger threatens, they either swim into, or are sucked up by, the parent's mouth.

Fishes

Left: A male seahorse broods the fertilized eggs in a pouch on his belly, and gives 'birth' 5 weeks later by contracting his body in jerks.
Right: A female, deep-sea angler fish with a parasitic male attached to her underside. His only function is to fertilize her eggs. This arrangement avoids the need to locate a partner in the dark sea depths.

Right: A mouthbrooding cichlid protects her eggs by carrying them in her mouth. Even after hatching, the young do not leave the shelter of her mouth until they are able to look after themselves.

Below: Niko Tinbergen, the German naturalist and ethnologist, made the first studies of the courtship of the 3-spined stickleback. Sign stimuli were shown to be the most important. A male will attack another male if it has a red throat and encroaches on his territory.

Red-bellied, blue-eyed male courts a female.

He leads her to his nest which he has built.

He nudges her gently to get her to lay her eggs.

She is now driven away from his nest.

He wriggles into the nest to fertilize the eggs.

The male guards and fans fresh water over the eggs.

drifting with the ocean currents back to the mouths of rivers.

In the breeding season many bony fishes, such as HERRINGS, haddock and cod, gather together in shoals. The females lay their eggs and the males shed milt or sperm onto the eggs and fertilize them. Millions of eggs die, with perhaps only one of those fertilized eggs developing into a mature adult fish. A female turbot, for example, produces about nine million eggs each breeding season.

Sticklebacks and fighting fish show more parental care and build nests for their eggs. Some fishes, such as the MOUTHBROODERS, carry their eggs inside the mouth. In the American CATFISH it is the male who does this. Male pipefishes and seahorses carry the fertilized eggs inside a special pouch on their belly. When the eggs have hatched, the male looks as if he is giving birth as he bends and stretches to eject the miniature seahorses from his pouch.

Female sharks and rays either give birth to live

P Pike are voracious carnivores, usually at the top of most freshwater food chains. The northern pike occurs in North America and Eurasia where it can grow to over a metre long and weigh about 20 kg.
Piranhas are small, South American freshwater fishes that immediately bring the word 'killer' to mind. Probably only 4 of the 20 or so species deserve this title. They mainly catch small fish, but if larger animals, such as a rodent like the capybara, get into difficulties in water, then hundreds will gather and quickly reduce the animal to a skeleton.
Plaice, see FLATFISHES.
Pufferfish have tiny mouths armed with heavy teeth and short, deep bodies that are often covered with spines. Most live over coral reefs. When pulled from the water they swallow air, or if threatened they will take in water. Thus they become balloon-shaped and are difficult for any predator to swallow. The porcupine puffer fish is covered with spines so that this forms an even more impenetrable barrier.

R Rays are flat-bodied cartilaginous fishes with large pectoral fins that are flapped in a wing-like fashion to move through the water. The stingrays and whiprays have venomous spines. The manta, or devil rays, are docile but huge, measuring up to 7 metres across the wing tips. The giant mantas are plankton feeders and do not attack man.
Remoras are fishes that have a sucker disk on the top of the head which has evolved from the dorsal fin. A remora uses this sucker to attach itself to fishes such as sharks, turtles and whales. It does not harm the host and takes parasitic crustaceans from the host's skin.

Porcupine pufferfish

S Salmon are popular fish with anglers because they put up a spectacular fight. They are hatched in

Fishes

Below right: The stonefish have venomous glands at the base of their spines. They lie perfectly camouflaged on the sea bed, and if a bather steps on one, poison is injected into the wound by the pressure of the foot on the bag-like glands. Effects vary from intense pain to cases of death occurring in 6 hours.

Right: The lateral lines on this tench are sense organs that run along the sides of its body. Along these lines, sensitive cells called neuromasts pick up pressure waves and translate them (via the brain) to indicate the direction and the size of the object producing the waves.

young, or lay a small number of eggs. These develop inside a horny, protective leather case.

The senses of fishes

The sense organs of fishes are not unlike those of higher vertebrates, but the adaptation to a water habitat means some are greatly accentuated while others are less developed. Most fishes have nostrils but these are never used for breathing purposes. They open into little sacs into which the water enters and can be smelt. Many fishes, such as sharks and piranha, hunt by smell, and salmon use smell to find their birthplaces.

Taste is another sense and it is closely linked to that of smell. Fishes have taste buds not only on their tongue but in many species, such as CARP and STURGEON, they are found on the head and body. CATFISH have tastebuds on the barbels that surround the mouth.

The eyes of fishes are adapted for underwater vision and are usually placed on the sides of the head. Very few fishes have binocular vision. The hammerheaded shark has its eyes at the ends of its 'hammer', and this probably improves its vision. One curious fish from Central America has eyes that stick out. Each eye is divided into two halves, the upper half is focused for seeing in air and the lower half for underwater.

Fishes hear vibrations in the water. The sound waves are sometimes magnified by the air bladder and carried to their inner ear. Fishes also have a sense organ which is not found in higher vertebrates. This is the lateral line system. It consists of a line of tiny pores along each side of the head and body. Nerves run to the brain from each pore and it seems that this system is nature's version of radar. When a fish swims near a rock, the vibrations sent out by the moving fish hit the rock, are reflected, and are picked up by the lateral line pores. This explains why blind cave fishes can move about in total darkness.

---

freshwater headstreams, migrate to sea and return several years later to spawn and then usually die.
Scorpion fish are also called dragonfish, turkey fish or lion fish. The name comes from the venomous nature of the long spines on their fins. The related stonefish is the most poisonous fish known.
Seahorses are strange fishes that move through the water with the body vertical. They have a bony armour and their horse-shaped head has a tubular snout. The female lays the eggs and the male broods them.
Sharks are some 200 species of cigar-shaped fishes, many of whom are predatory and some are man-eaters. Whale sharks and basking sharks are the largest living fishes, reaching almost 20 metres; they feed on plankton.
Sticklebacks are small, aggressive fishes with armoured bony plates down the sides of the body. They also have spines on the dorsal ridge. In the breeding season the male develops a bright red belly and constructs a nest. He attracts a female by a zig-zag dance. The female lays her eggs in his nest and the male immediately fertilizes them and then chases her away. He brings up the young fishes alone.
Stonefish, see SCORPION FISH.
Sturgeons are fishes of northern temperate waters that can grow to almost 1,000 kg. They have 5 rows of plate-like scales along the sides of their bodies. Sturgeon's eggs are made into caviar.

Trout are closely related to SALMON and are usually restricted to fresh waters although some, such as the sea trout, migrate between sea and river.

Scorpion fish

Shovel-nosed sturgeon

Arthropods are the most numerous of all animals. They include insects — the largest animal class of all — crustaceans, arachnids, centipedes and millipedes. The number of recorded insects is increasing as new species are discovered.

Arthropods

Members of the arthropod (jointed limbs) group are the most numerous and widespread in numbers of species and individuals. They are the only invertebrate group to have successfully adapted to living on land and include the only other animals, apart from the vertebrate birds and bats, to have become modified for flight. More than 800,000 species have been described for this group and this is about 80 per cent of all known animal species.

All these animals, whether LOBSTER, CENTIPEDE or BEETLE have a hard shell that forms an outer skeleton (the exoskeleton). The shell is rather like a suit of armour in that it is jointed and the muscles are arranged across the joints so that the parts of the exoskeleton are able to move in relation to each other. The shell is almost impermeable to water in both directions. This is very important to those arthropods on land, especially the large group of INSECTS, as it prevents them from drying out.

One disadvantage of the shell is that it restricts growth, and the developing arthropod is always outgrowing it. Every so often the shell is shed or moulted. Usually the animal splits its old cuticle (skin) and then pulls itself out. A new cuticle has already grown and while it is relatively soft and pliable, the animal stretches and increases in size. Shortly afterwards, the cuticle hardens and again becomes an armour-like exoskeleton. No further increase in size takes place until the next moult. When an arthropod has just moulted it is in great danger as it is defenceless with a 'naked' body, and also it cannot move very far.

Movement of the millions

Some arthropods such as BEES, dragonflies and lacewings, all of which are insects, are great fliers. Others like spiders and silverfish move around on the ground on their jointed legs. There are also thousands that live and move about in

Crustacea: Lobster
Arachnida: Scorpion 
Insecta: Grasshopper 
Merostomata: King crab 
Symphyla: Symphylan 
Thysanura: Silverfish 
Onychophora: Velvet worm 
Collembola: Springtail 
Diplopoda: Millipede 
Pauropoda: Pauropod 
Diplura: Bristletail 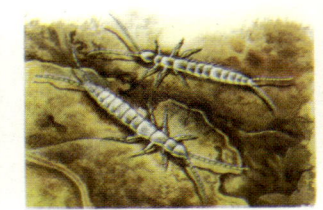
Chilopoda: Centipede 
Protura: Proturan 

Above: The arthropods form the largest phylum in the animal kingdom, containing more than 800,000 species. All the animals in the 13 classes have their bodies divided into segments and have an outer skeleton called the cuticle.

Reference

A Ant lions are large INSECTS that look rather like dragonflies. The larvae dig little sand pits and hide at the bottom. When a spider or ant walks too near the steep-sided pit it slips down to be gripped by the waiting jaws. These jaws inject a paralysing poison into the victim's body; it is then sucked dry.
Ants are social INSECTS of the order Hymenoptera. They are more numerous than any other land animal. Colonies may contain from a few dozen to thousands. There are 3 castes: queens, males and workers.
Aphids, or greenfly, are very small, soft-bodied insects of the order Homoptera. Both winged and wingless forms exist. Most species have piercing beaks that can extract plant sap.
Arachnida. This very varied class contains the SPIDERS, SCORPIONS, TICKS, MITES, HARVESTMEN and whip scorpions.
Arthropoda. This phylum includes PERIPATUS, CRUSTACEANS, CENTIPEDES, MILLIPEDES,

Aphid

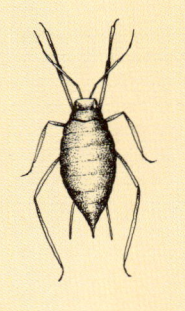

SPIDERS, horseshoe crabs, sea spiders, and INSECTS. They are all segmented and have hard exoskeletons.

B Barnacles are marine CRUSTACEANS and live attached to hard surfaces such as rocks, ship bottoms, and even whales. There are 2 kinds. The conical species have protective plates surrounding the body and are common on inter-tidal rocks. The other type are the goose barnacles. These have flattened shells and a long neck or stalk. They feed on plankton which they catch with their feathery legs.
Bees are members of the order Hymenoptera which includes ANTS and WASPS. They feed their young on pollen and nectar (honey), the pollen being collected in pollen baskets on their legs. Bees are very important agents for pollinating flowers. Honey bees and bumble bees are social insects. A colony contains 1 queen (a female), a few drones (males), and many workers (sexually underdeveloped females). Many bees are solitary, such as leafcutter bees and mining bees.
Beetles are the largest order (Coleoptera) of INSECTS. More than 300,000 species inhabit almost every available habitat in the world.

40 Arthropods

Above: A beautiful swallowtail butterfly. It gets its name from the tail-like extensions of the hind wings.

Right: A vertical take-off by a green lacewing showing its controlled manoeuvres and delicately veined wing membranes.

water, such as crabs, lobsters, water beetles and copepods, and their legs have adapted for this life.

In arthropods, the number of legs varies and some have become modified for other functions. In a few cases the number is as few as two pairs, as in a preying mantis, but most insects use three pairs of legs and spiders use four pairs. CRABS, although they have five pairs of legs, use only three in crawling sideways, the other pairs being claws adapted for feeding and grasping, and for swimming. Water beetles have flattened, paddle-shaped legs for swimming, while the third pair of legs in FLEAS and GRASSHOPPERS have become specialized for jumping.

Insects first flew some 200 million years before reptiles and birds took to the air. Over 320 million years ago in the Carboniferous period there were immense dragonfly-like creatures with a wingspan of up to 76 centimetres.

Insect wings are attached to the THORAX via couplings that act like a series of ball and socket joints. This enables the animal to fly sideways, backwards, upside down, swoop, climb vertically

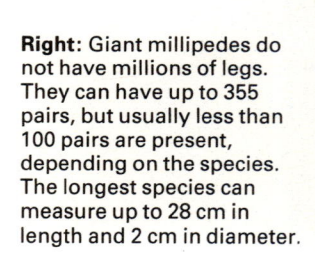

Right: Giant millipedes do not have millions of legs. They can have up to 355 pairs, but usually less than 100 pairs are present, depending on the species. The longest species can measure up to 28 cm in length and 2 cm in diameter.

They range in size from the microscopic fungus beetle to the gigantic tropical atlas and hercules beetle.

Bristletails are small- to medium-sized wingless insects with 3 bristles at the tip of the abdomen. They have chewing mouthparts for feeding on decaying plant material.

Bugs belong to the order Hemiptera which means 'half wing'; only half of the front pair of wings is thickened. They have piercing and sucking mouthparts and can do great damage to plants on which they feed.

White admiral butterfly

Butterflies, together with MOTHS, form the large insect order Lepidoptera, which contains more than 120,000 species. Many beautiful and large specimens are collected and have now become rare. Butterflies have clubbed antennae and fly during sunny periods of the day. They undergo complete metamorphosis – from egg, larva or caterpillar, pupa or chrysalis, to adult.

Centipedes, of the class Chilopoda, have flattened bodies with a pair of legs on each segment, except for the last two. There are some 5,000 species in the world.

Chilopoda, see CENTIPEDES.

Cicadas are more often heard than seen. These 1,500 species of insect sing to each other by vibrating a small drum-like membrane. They are the largest members of the order Homoptera.

Cockroaches are very ancient insects, with most of the 3,500 living species coming from the tropics. They have flat bodies and long, slender running legs. They hide in cracks by day

Male cockroach

and come out to feed at night.

Crabs, of the class Crustacea, are relatives of the

Arthropods 41

and hover. Power is applied in different ways depending on the species but usually comes from two pairs of large muscles.

How arthropods feed

Within the arthropod grouping almost every conceivable material is used as a food source by one or more insect groups. There are fish-feeders, plankton-feeders, wood-feeders, blood-feeders, dung-feeders and sap-feeders to name but a few.

Some limbs have been modified to act as feeding organs. These lie on or close to the head. The pincers of crabs and scorpions catch the food, while other limbs break it up and pass it to the mouth. Beetles, ants, wasps, grasshoppers, locusts, earwigs and dragonflies on the whole have biting mouthparts, with jaws or mandibles to cut and crush the food. All true BUGS and flies, as well as most butterflies and moths, have sucking mouths but the actual structure of the mouthparts varies. Houseflies are only able to suck up liquid food. BUTTERFLIES and moths that feed on the nectar of flowers have a tubular mouth (proboscis) which is coiled up under the head when not in use. It unrolls and acts rather like a drinking straw when the insect is feeding. Bugs, such as greenfly, have sharp piercing mouthparts to suck up the sap from a plant's tissues. MOSQUITOES and fleas pierce their victim, usually a mammal or bird with their needle-shaped jaws and then suck up the blood.

SPIDERS are mainly carnivorous. They usually capture victims, usually small insects or other arthropods, by a web or trap. Enzymes, secreted by the spider, are injected into the prey and its tissues are broken down so that it can then be sucked up by the spider's mouth. Some spiders possess fangs which inject poison into their prey to paralyse or kill it.

Group behaviour

The behaviour of arthropods is extremely varied but basically it is designed to ensure the species survives in order to reproduce. Most behaviour is instinctive, the behaviour patterns being passed on from generation to generation. A limited amount of learning is possible in some insects. Cockroaches can be trained to go right or left by punishing them when a wrong turn is made.

In the insects we find the most highly-

Above: A grasshopper's mouthparts *(top)* are designed for cutting. A butterfly's tube *(right)* sucks up nectar, and a mosquito *(bottom)* has a bloodsucking tube.

Left: A female garden spider is seen here eating her mate. In the animal world, the female of the species is often deadlier than the male.

Above: The ticks on this little wood mouse have swollen up by feeding on their host's blood. They leave their host only to breed.

LOBSTER. They usually run sideways or 'crab-wise', although they are able to move in any direction. Although mainly seashore or marine in habitat, a few live in freshwater. Their pincers are used for feeding, defence and courtship.
Crayfish are freshwater lobsters found mainly in temperate streams and rivers.
Crustaceans include SHRIMPS, prawns, LOBSTERS, crayfish, CRABS, BARNACLES and krill (the food of baleen whales). The 26,000 species are mainly marine or freshwater.

Krill

D Daddy-long-legs, see HARVESTMAN SPIDER.
Diplopoda, see MILLIPEDES.

F Fiddler crabs live mainly in the tropics. The males have one absurdly big claw, termed the fiddle, which is used for defence and courtship. Females have no fiddle.
Fleas are small wingless INSECTS that feed on the blood of warm-blooded mammals and birds. They have a compressed body covered with spines that point backwards, thus allowing them to move freely between an animal's feathers or hair. An infested animal may have many thousands of fleas on its body at any one time. The majority of the 1,800 species live in the tropics.
Flies are INSECTS with only one pair of wings. They are very numerous and widespread. They show complete metamorphosis, the larvae often being called maggots.

G Grasshoppers, totalling over 10,000 species, are either short- or long-horned. Each species has its own distinctive sound. Shorthorns make their sound by rubbing the femur of their hind leg against the hardened area on the front wing. Longhorns rub their front wings together.
Greenfly, see APHIDS.

H Harvestman spiders are seen most often at harvest time, and are often termed daddy-long-legs.
Horseshoe crabs, or king crabs, are neither crabs nor CRUSTACEANS. They are ARACHNIDS, the group to which spiders and scorpions belong. Their bodies are pro-

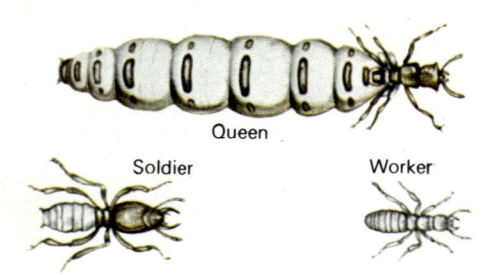

42 Arthropods

Left: Termite society is divided into workers, soldiers and the colony's king and queen.
Below: Air in the living quarters of the termite mud nest is heated by the activity of millions of workers. This air rises to the top of the nest. Here fresh, cooler air enters from the outside and circulates down the nest.

organized social behaviour. Although the majority of insect species lead solitary lives, two groups are social. These are the TERMITES, or white ants, of the order Isoptera and the BEES, wasps and ANTS of the order Hymenoptera. Here parents and offspring live together in a community in one nest and actually co-operate in running the home. An ant colony is headed by a queen, with various castes (groups), such as soldiers or workers, performing different tasks.

Many moths and butterflies migrate thousands of kilometres annually to escape harsh climatic conditions and food shortages. The most famous and well-tracked insect migration is that of the monarch butterfly of America. LOCUSTS build up to plague numbers and move off as a swarm in a certain direction, devastating all the vegetation in their path, but do not return. This one-way movement is called emigration.

Life cycles and reproducing

In most arthropod species there is a different set of instinctive behaviour patterns for the two sexes. The female's role is to deposit and protect the eggs. Courtship displays, where the sexes come together for mating, are brief. A male fiddler crab waves his huge claw to attract a female. Many jumping spiders wave their legs and dance from side to side to attract a mate. A small male preying mantis when attempting to mate with his chosen larger female must approach with great caution or he will get his head bitten off by the predatory female.

Like most invertebrates, arthropods lay large numbers of small eggs. Usually the young hatch at an immature stage and must feed to grow and develop further. The larvae of aquatic species are free-swimming and undergo a gradual change into an adult. Caterpillar larvae are so different from the adult butterfly that it is not possible to have a gradual change. A larva surrounds itself

---

tected by an armour-plated shell and they have survived almost unchanged for 500 million years.

Insects account for about 80 per cent of all the known kinds of animals. There exist almost 1 million species. Some beetles and midges are the size of a pin head while stick insects can measure about 30 cm, and some moths have a wingspan this size. The presence of wings is the best way of distinguishing insects from other arthropods, although lice and FLEAS have lost

Hercules beetle

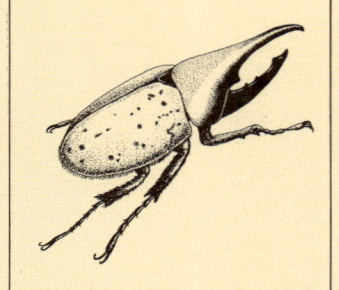

theirs. The head has one pair of antennae and 3 pairs of mouthparts. The 3-segmented thorax has a pair of legs on each segment. The abdomen has 11 segments.

Ladybirds are useful BEETLES which feed on pests, such as APHIDS. Most of the 5,000 species are yellow, orange or red with black spots.

Lobsters are large CRUSTACEANS, related to shrimps. Young lobsters look like small shrimps. Later they develop huge pincer claws, settle on the sea bed and become scavengers.

Locusts are destructive short-horned GRASSHOPPERS. Each continent has one or more species of locust that at times builds up an enormous population that then migrates in incredible swarms. The reasons why are still not fully understood.

Ladybird

Merostomata. This class contains the HORSESHOE CRABS.
Millipedes, of the class Diplopoda are ARTHROPODS with a horny outer layer that forms a hard armour that is used for burrowing. They usually have more legs than CENTIPEDES, although the longest has no more than 200 legs. The 8,000 species worldwide are usually vegetarian.
Mites are related to TICKS, and are quite tiny. Most species live in leaf litter. Segmentation typical of ARTHROPODS is reduced or absent. They have four pairs

Fresh air
Stale air

Arthropods

with a protective material and transforms itself into a pupa. This is referred to as its 'quiescent' stage, and indeed it is externally. After a time a sexually mature adult emerges. These changes are termed metamorphosis, which means change in form. In the many insects that go through this process, there is a marked division of labour among the different phases of the life history. A caterpillar hatches complete with chewing jaws and immediately starts to feed on leaves. Its role is feeding and in a short time it has eaten large quantities of food and grown quite rapidly. The pupal resting stage is the transformation stage. The winged adult butterfly that emerges has no biting or chewing jaws but sucks nectar with its coiled tubular mouth. Its chief adult role is to distribute the species by flying to new and suitable habitats and finding a mate. Some adults do not even feed, mating soon after emerging from a pupa and dying when the eggs have been laid.

Some primitive insects, such as silverfish, hatch out as small-scale replicas of their parents. They grow to adult size by feeding and moulting. In COCKROACHES and LOCUSTS, a nymph hatches out of the egg. It looks like a miniature adult, except that its wings are undeveloped. As it grows and moults the wings gradually become more identified until the fully mature stage is attained. This sequence of egg-nymph-adult is known as incomplete metamorphosis.

Left: The peacock butterfly's life cycle is an example of complete metamorphosis. This is where the egg hatches into a form entirely different from the adult. This larva, or caterpillar, passes through a pupal or chrysalis stage where it changes into the adult form.

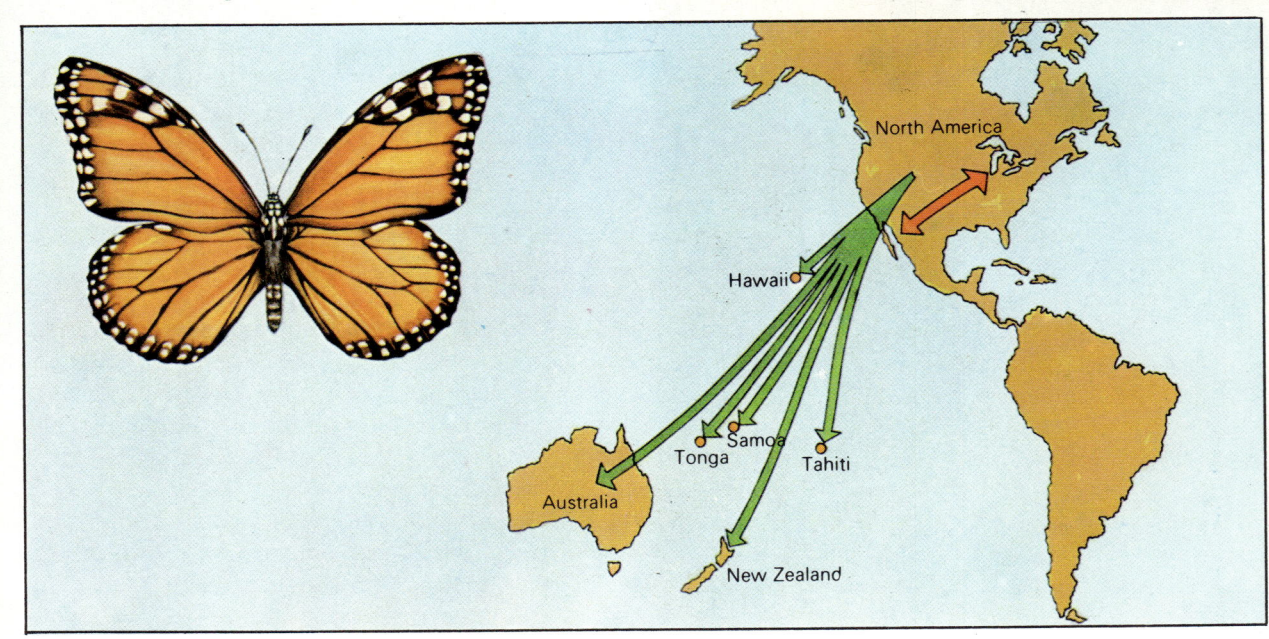

Above: Malayan fiddler crabs defend their small territories of sand by signalling with their large claw. The claw is also used in courtship displays.

Left: The North American monarch butterfly is one of the few species of insects that make annual 2-way journeys comparable to the distances covered by some birds. Some travel over 3,000 km between their summer breeding places and winter feeding ranges in the south. In the last 130 years the butterfly has expanded its range westwards across the Pacific, probably using ships for rides.

---

of legs.

Mosquitoes inflict more direct harm to man than any other known INSECT. The 2,000 species are distributed worldwide. A mosquito female needs a meal of blood after mating and before she lays her eggs. When they bite man, diseases such as malaria and yellow fever can be transmitted. Control methods, such as chemical spraying or draining the breeding sites, have had some success.

Moths, together with BUTTERFLIES, belong to the insect order Lepidoptera. Most moths are nocturnal. The males have hairy bodies and feathery antennae. At rest the wings are held horizontally and not vertically as in butterflies.

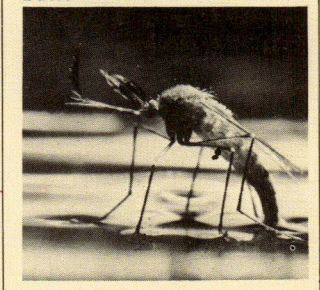

Mosquito

P Pauropoda. This class contains tiny ARTHROPODS about 1 mm long that live mainly in the soil.

Peripatus is a velvet worm of the class Onychophora. It lives under logs and stones in the tropics and is up to 15 mm long.

Proturans are the class that contain tiny 12-segmented animals about 1 mm long that are found in leaf litter. They use their fore-legs as feelers.

S Scorpions are related to spiders and are most abundant in the warmer regions of the world. Some measure about 15 cm in length. The tip of the abdomenal tail has a powerful poison gland which stings or paralyses enemies or prey. Prey are then sucked dry of their juices.

Hawk moth

Arthropods

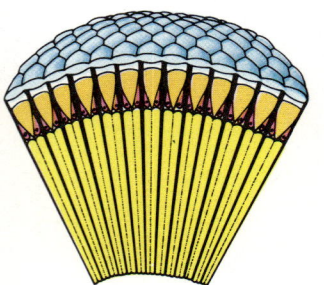

Left: A cross-section of an insect's compound eye. Each facet consists of a tiny lens, a light-transmitting system and sensitive retinal cells. Each facet registers a fragment of the total picture seen so that the whole eye builds up a jigsaw mozaic of the scene. It is probably a blurred image because insects cannot focus.

Above: The prominent compound eyes of a bluebottle are seen here. Each eye is made up of about 4,000 6-sided facets.

Below: The feathery feelers of this male Thailand Atlas moth can trace the scent of a female up to a kilometre or more away.

Senses of arthropods

The most important sense of a species depends on the kind of life it leads. CRUSTACEANS and insects are arthropods that have a pair of compound eyes. Most of the other arthropods have only simple eyes. Actually, most insects possess both simple and compound eyes. Simple eyes have no focusing mechanism but probably only measure light intensity. A compound eye is composed of hundreds or even thousands of light-condensing units. It does not give as good an image as the human eye. Insects probably see images similar to a human being looking at a newspaper photograph through a magnifying glass. The compound eye can detect the slightest movement of an enemy or prey.

Smell bring the sexes together, finds suitable egg-laying sites or food, and often enables a species to identify its own kind. Male MOTHS use their feathery sensory antennae to home in on female moths that are giving off chemical scents. They can locate a female up to three kilometres away. Social insects, such as ants or bees, can not only detect members of their own species but can sniff out and attack an intruder from a rival colony.

Taste receptors occur mainly in the mouth and mouthparts, at the tip of the antennae and on the lower parts of the legs. When a fly lands on your jam sandwich he is actually tasting the food with his feet!

Hearing is unequally developed in the arthropod group. Many species are probably deaf, although the insects are the best equipped at hearing. Their range covers a wider frequency band than that to which the human ear is sensitive. The 'ears' of an insect are either sensitive hairs, or tympanal organs situated on the first abdominal segment. When a sound hits this tympanal organ, an air sac beneath it transmits the vibrations to the brain.

Sea spiders are a small marine group of the class Pycnogonida that have long narrow bodies and 4 to 7 pairs of legs. They are not true spiders.

Shrimps are CRUSTACEANS, closely related to prawns and lobsters. They are active swimmers finding food mainly by scavenging.

Spider crabs are peculiar CRUSTACEANS with long legs. Their body is often covered with warts or spines. The giant spider crab from Japan may measure more than 3 metres across the claws, and is the largest crustacean.

Spiders belong to the class Arachnida and are widespread, ranging in size from less than 1 mm to 25 mm long. They have chelicerae that bear poison fangs, and have silk glands in their abdomen. Four pairs of long legs are attached to the abdomen. Many species have excellent sight.

T**ermites** are often called 'white ants' although they are not ANTS at all. Ants have a waist between the thorax and abdomen whereas the join is broader in termites. These social insects build huge colony mounds up to 10 metres high.

Thorax is the second of the three sections of an INSECT. It bears the legs and wings.

Ticks are closely related to MITES and belong to the Arachnida class. They are all parasitic at some stage in their lives. They gorge themselves on blood and often transmit diseases.

Leaf-curling spider

W**asps** belong to the same order of INSECTS, the Hymenoptera, as ANTS and bees. Many species are social but some are solitary, such as the potter wasps.

Wood lice are land CRUSTACEANS, their bodies being protected by hard plates. When certain species are disturbed they are able to roll into a ball, like tiny armadillos. They prefer damp places and come out to feed at night.

The invertebrate world includes many other species besides the arthropods. They range from the simplest animals—microscopic protozoans, which some botanists claim are plants – to the giant squid and the Portuguese man-o'-war.

Other Invertebrates

Protozoa: Flagellate
Porifera: Bath sponge 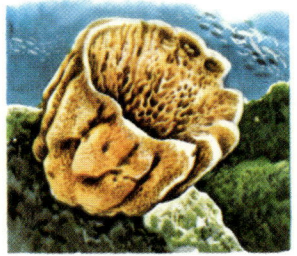
Coelenterata: Portuguese man-o'-war  
Platyhelminthes: Liverfluke 
Aschelminthes: Roundworm 
Mollusca: Edible snail 
Annelida: Earthworm 
Echinodormata: Sun starfish 
Hemichordata: Acorn worm 
Tunicata: Sea squirt 
Nemertina: Ribbon worm
Brachiopoda: Lamp shell

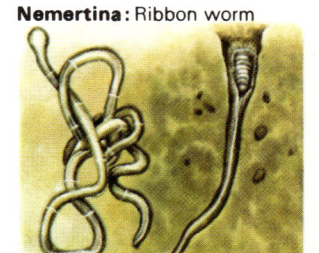

Above: The numerous species in the various invertebrate phyla illustrated above have adapted to fill various niches in water or on land. Some species, such as the lamp shells, are survivors from the past while others such as the molluscs are very numerous and successful all over the world. The tunicates and hemichordates link the invertebrates with the vertebrates.

The previous chapter mainly dealt with the jointed-legged arthropods, but the invertebrate world exhibits an enormous variety of animal life. Other groups include the PROTOZOANS, microscopic SPONGES, JELLYFISH, FLATWORMS, ringworms, snails, worms and STARFISH.

The simple, single-celled *protozoa* play an important part alongside microscopic plants in aquatic habitats, by providing the basis for all food chains in the sea. The many-celled sponges evolved from colonies of single-celled protozoans, but the former is not a very successful group, mainly because they have no nervous system linking the activities of various parts of the body. The COELENTERATES and flatworms are more advanced because they have evolved a simple nervous system. These groups also show the beginnings of a digestive system. The segmented ANNELIDS (worms) are adapted for swimming and burrowing. They have a better developed nervous and blood system.

A major invertebrate group is the MOLLUSCA, most of which have a heavy shell and are slow-moving, for example garden snails.

There is a strange assortment of creatures at the more complex end of the invertebrate scale. The ECHINODERMS are very distinctively symmetrical, including the familiar starfish, BRITTLE STARS, feather stars, sea urchins and SEA CUCUMBERS. They all have spiny skins and the five-rayed star pattern can be found in almost all the species. The primitive tunicates and HEMICHORDATES are closer to the vertebrates than the invertebrates because in the larval stage in their life they possess a rod of inflated cells (the notochord) that acts as a support for the body, thus showing some similarity to the spinal column in vertebrates.

Senses and movement
Sense organs and methods of movement in the numerous groups vary according to their habitat

Reference

A **Amoeba,** a single-celled PROTOZOAN, is often incorrectly thought of as being the simplest form of life living today. It lives mainly in water but is sometimes found as a parasite in man.
Annelids, or worms, have their muscular segmented bodies covered in a thin skin and bristles. There are over 6,800 species in the 3 classes (BRISTLEWORMS, EARTHWORMS, and LEECHES).
Aschelminthes are unsegmented animals such as the rotifers, roundworms and hairworms. They all have an alimentary canal with a mouth and anus.

B **Bivalves** are some 8,000 species of flattened MOLLUSCS that consist of 2 rounded, oval or elongated hinged shells in which the soft-bodied animal lives. Large gills filter their food from ocean currents. Many species use their muscular foot to burrow with. Others, such as mussels, attach themselves firmly to rocks with long, sticky threads.
Brittle stars are ECHINODERMS that are star-shaped but have very slender arms radiating from a small central disc-shaped body. They feed on plankton.
Bristleworms, or ragworms, are marine ANNELIDS that have numerous bristles growing from muscular, fleshy 'paddles' called parapodia.

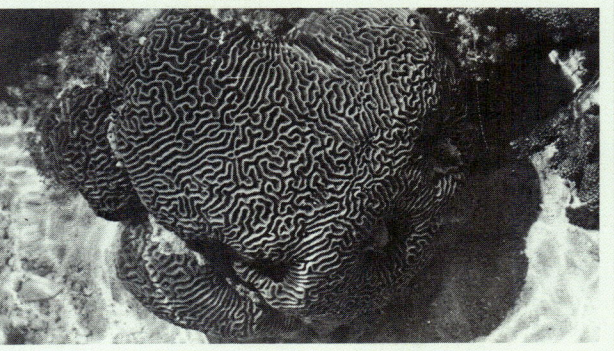

Brain coral

C **Coelenterates** are the aquatic group that contains the HYDROIDS, JELLYFISH, SEA ANEMONES and CORALS. They are the most primitive of the many-celled animals. Tentacles, placed round the mouth, bear cells that can seize, sting and paralyse prey. There are 2 basic struc-

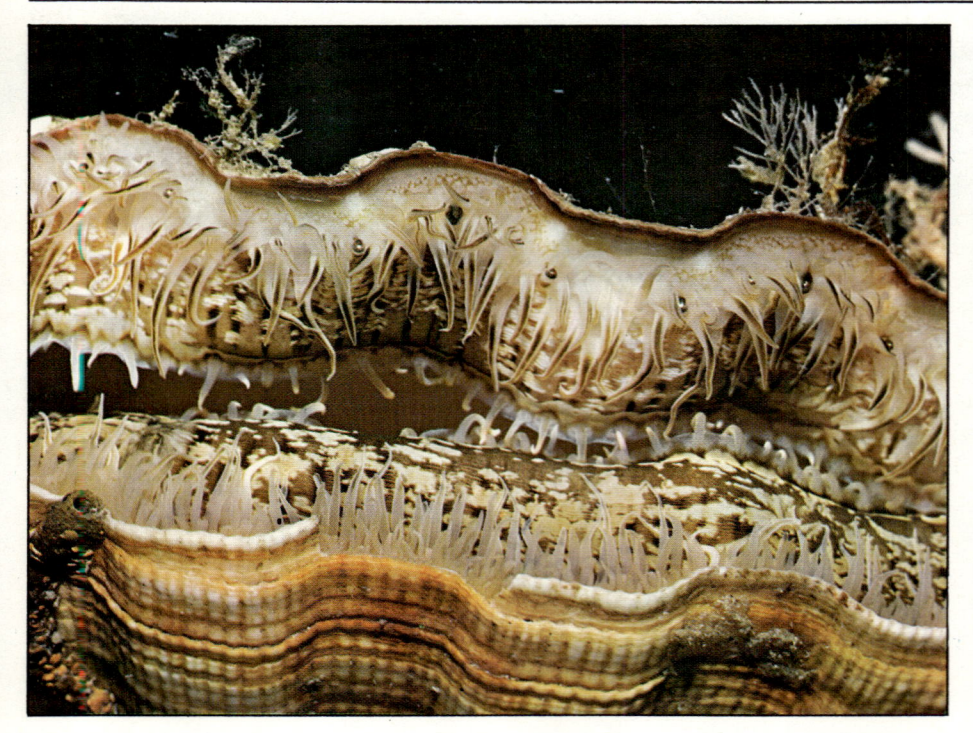

Other Invertebrates

and the lives they lead. Most of the primitive protozoans push themselves along by vibrating long flagella, or smaller hair-like structures called 'cilia'. AMOEBAS push out a portion of their body, towards which the rest of their body flows. They cannot see but are sensitive to light intensity and chemical changes in their surroundings.

The coelenterates, such as the jellyfish and the SEA ANEMONES, have tentacles that are sensitive to touch. The Portuguese man-o'-war, for example, has tentacles and POLYPS which grow to about two metres long. A fish swimming into this dangling mass is almost immediately stunned by the stinging cells and drawn towards the feeding polyps.

The senses of touch and sight are well developed in some species of molluscs. Land snails have two pairs of tentacles on their heads. The smaller, front pair, are thought to be concerned with the sense of smell and the larger pair carry eyes on the tips. Water snails tend to have only one pair of tentacles and the eyes are at the base. The most highly evolved and intelligent molluscs are the SQUIDS, CUTTLEFISH, and OCTOPUSES. The eight-armed octopus has excellent eyesight comparable to that of a vertebrate. Other much simpler eyes (or 'ocelli') are found in the BIVALVES (two-shelled molluscs) such as scallops and clams. These 'eyes' cannot focus but are very sensitive to light intensity.

Land SNAILS and SLUGS walk on a muscular foot, but the foot has evolved to become flapping wings in the sea butterflies. In some bivalves, such as oysters, the muscular foot is used to drag themselves around but in the scallops, they move by clapping the two halves of the shell together and forcing out the water. As with all bivalves, these molluscs feed on tiny particles suspended in the water or lying on the sea bed. The particles are filtered through the gills of the breathing organs and passed to the mouth.

The echinoderms

The spiny-skinned ECHINODERMS, such as starfish, are often found on the sea shore. These animals have a system of water-filled canals that run through the body. Tiny branches protrude from the skin and are known as tube feet. These are used for movement and respiration. In the starfish, the suction effect of the tube feet is used to open the shells of oysters and mussels. Then the starfish push out their stomachs over the mollusc and secrete digestive stomach juices. The semi-liquid food is sucked up and passed into digestive glands in the arms.

The globular sea urchins are without arms but they also have tube feet in the five rays around

Above: Around the mantle edge of the scallop are located numerous bright blue 'eyes'. Each 'eye' has a lens, cornea and retina but probably cannot see an image. It can detect sudden changes in light intensity.

Right: An octopus swims by rapidly expelling water from the mantle cavity through a funnel.

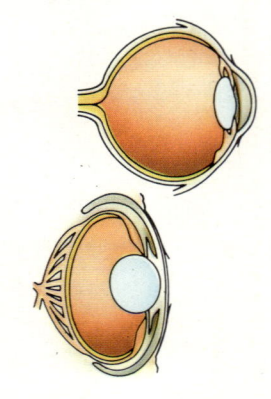

Above: An octopus's eye (*bottom*) focuses by changing the length between lens and retina, not by changing the lens shape as in a human eye (*top*).

---

tures: the cylindrical POLYPS, such as anemones, hydroids and coral, attached to rocks, and the free-swimming jellyfish.
Corals, closely related to SEA ANEMONES, are COELENTERATES growing in colonies. Their POLYPS are protected by a hard external skeleton composed of calcium carbonate. Coral reefs are formed by millions of these polyps continuously budding.
Cuttlefish are molluscs with both eyes and an internal shell – the cuttlebone. Like their relatives the SQUIDS and OCTOPUSES, they have an ink sac near the anus. When alarmed they release the ink to form a dense smoke-screen to enable them to escape.

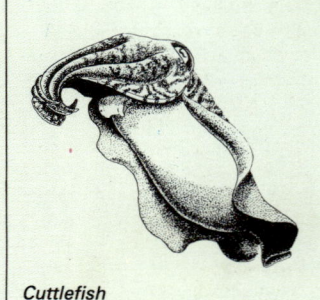

Cuttlefish

E **Earthworms** range in length from just a few centimetres to over 3 metres. Although they are ANNELIDS, they have just a few bristles and lack parapodia (feet-like projections). They have both male and female sex organs, but certain mechanisms ensure that cross-fertilization takes place.
Echinodermata are marine animals such as the radially symmetrical STARFISH, BRITTLE STARS, sea urchins, SEA CUCUMBERS and feather stars. Most adults can move by means of tube feet, but only very slowly. The spiny skin gives some protection.

F **Flatworms** are members of the group PLATYHELMINTHES, the majority of which are parasitic, such as flukes and tapeworms. Flatworms are aquatic animals. Most species are less than 2 cm long. They show remarkable powers of regeneration when body parts are lost.

H **Hemichordata** are marine animals such as acorn worms. They are the most primitive of the chordates as they possess a notochord (the forerunner to the backbone).
Hydroids are some 2,700 species of COELENTERATES including *Hydra* and *Obelia*. They usually alternate between a POLYP and a free-swimming stage during their life cycle. Many of the marine growths on rock and shells are hydroid colonies.

J **Jellyfish,** of which there are some 200 species, spend the major part of their lives free-swimming in the oceans of the world. They swim by pulsating their

the body. Their shell is rigid due to skeletal plates but there are holes through which the tube feet pass. The sea urchin is equipped with five strong beak-like teeth worked by a series of muscles. This equipment is used to chew food such as seaweed or dead sea creatures.

The annelids

The ANNELIDS, or ringed worms, live in all types of soil except acidic sandy ones. They are valuable assets to gardeners and farmers because they feed on decaying plant and animal matter, and their tunnelling helps soil cultivation by allowing air and water to reach the soil. Charles DARWIN (see page 4) studied earthworms and estimated that every particle of topsoil goes through a worm at least once every few years.

Most bristleworms live in mud or sand burrows on the ocean bed, filtering particles from the ocean currents using their long tentacles. The ragworms are wanderers, using their side feet known as 'parapodia' to move over the sea bed or swim along. The ragworm has two horny jaws for gripping prey.

The leeches are parasitic annelids. Some feed on small animals while others just suck blood and other juices from larger animals. At one end a leech is usually equipped with a large sucker with which it attaches itself to a host. The mouth opens in the middle of the sucker and some species have teeth.

Corals – the reef builders

The beautiful coral reefs that are found in warm, shallow tropical seas are the results of the work of millions of tiny relatives of the SEA ANEMONES, the corals. Each animal varies from a millimetre to about two centimetres in length and forms a limestone skeleton around its anemone-like body. These limestone skeletons form the basis of the coral reef. The many different coral species form their own shapes such as brain coral.

Below: This mollusc, a bivalve, looks rather immobile when resting on the bottom of the sea bed. However, if a predatory starfish approaches, the scallop takes quick evasive action to avoid being eaten. It moves by snapping its 2 shells together, thus expelling water.

Below: A Portuguese man-o'-war has here trapped and killed a fish in its mass of stinging tentacles.

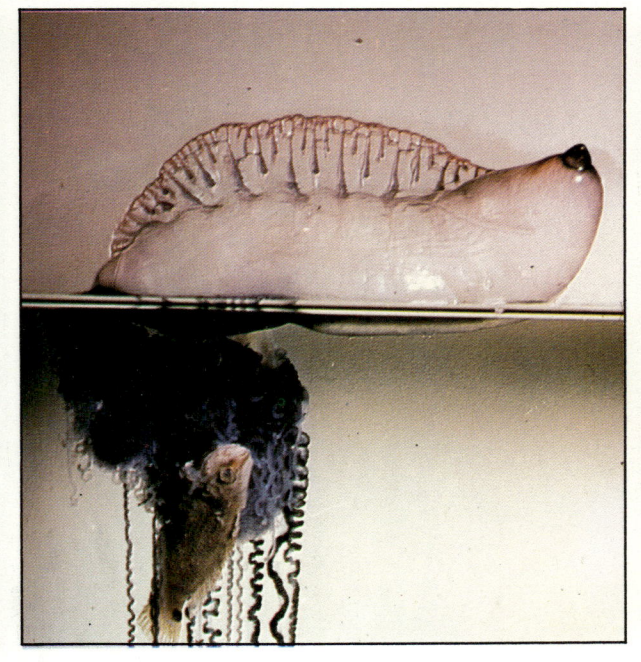

Below: Most spectacular and beautiful of all molluscs, sea slugs breathe through their colourful feathery projections, the cerata, growing from the dorsal surface. The species illustrated is found in the tropical coral reefs off Mozambique.

---

bell and this can range in size from a few millimetres to 2 metres across.

L **Leeches** are some 300 species of parasitic ANNELIDS that have few segments, no bristles or parapodia and a much reduced body cavity. Most species are aquatic and cling to their plant or animal hosts by suckers which are found at both ends of the body.

M **Mollusca** are animals with unsegmented bodies, such as SNAILS, BIVALVES, and SQUIDS, and highly developed blood and nervous systems. They do not have a standard shape, the body outline depending on the environment in which the species lives. Most molluscs, except the highly-evolved OCTOPUS group, are slow movers.

O **Octopuses** are fast moving, highly-evolved molluscs, closely related to squids and cuttlefish. They possess a very efficient nervous system and eyes. The mollusc shell has been lost during the course of evolution. It moves by either pulling itself over the rocks by 8 suckered tentacles or arms, or by forcibly expelling water from its funnel.

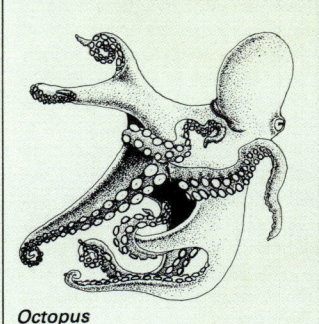

P **Platyhelminthes** are the FLATWORMS, flukes and tapeworms, a large group of some 5,500 species.
Polyp is the adult individual of some multicellular organisms such as HYDROIDS. It is either attached by its base to a solid anchorage or forms part of a floating colony.
Porifera are some 5,000 species of SPONGES. They are mainly marine, only a small minority being freshwater-dwelling and they are able to reproduce sexually and asexually.
Protozoa is the large group of over 30,000 species of simple single-celled animals, although this cell is often highly specialized. Most species are microscopic such as AMOEBA and the parasite, plasmodium.

Pelagia colorata (jellyfish)

Octopus

Reproduction

In the invertebrate world there are many ways of producing young. An AMOEBA, for example, can reproduce by simply splitting into two, a division termed 'binary fission'. In coelenterates such as *Obelia*, *Hydra* (HYDROIDS) or SEA ANEMONES, new individuals can be produced by budding. A few cells of the parent separate off and form a bud (a perfect miniature of the adult). This new bud then breaks away to grow into a mature adult animal.

Some lower forms of life reproduce by fragmentation. This occurs where an animal's body breaks up into two or more parts, as in some species of aquatic worm. In part of the jellyfish life cycle, a larva that has been produced sexually by swimming adults is released, settles on a rock, and grows into a sea-anemone-like animal. This grows up in layers, each layer becoming an eight-armed bud, called an 'ephyra', which eventually breaks off and develops into an adult jellyfish.

The majority of higher invertebrates reproduce sexually although there is a great deal of wastage and many die in their early stages. Sexual reproduction takes place in some animals that can also reproduce asexually, for example the *Hydra*. A simple type of sexual reproduction occurs in many single-celled protozoans. Here two individuals fuse side by side and exchange material from their nuclei. However, higher invertebrates usually have male and female sex cells, although one individual may have both. Snails and earthworms, for example, possess both male and female sex cells. The eggs of a pair of mating earthworms, for example, are each fertilized by the other's male cells. Starfish shed their eggs and sperm into the sea-water in huge numbers. Fertilization thus takes place very much by chance.

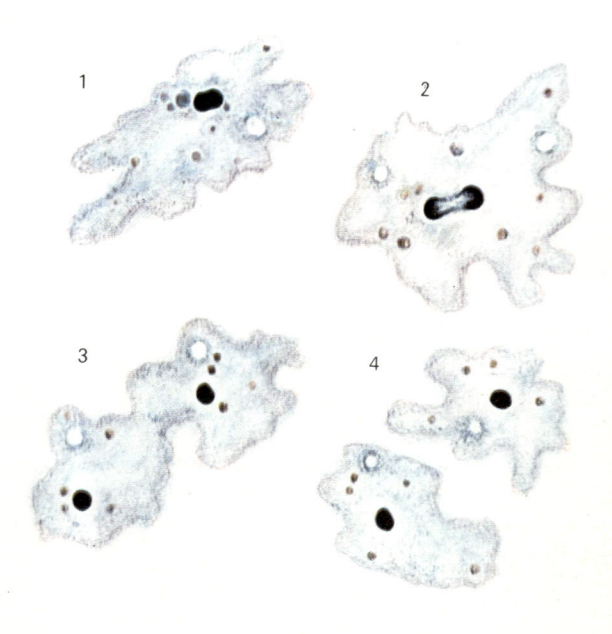

Above: Although snails have both male and female sex organs, they mate and cross fertilize one another. Prior to copulation, a pair of snails indulge in a very peculiar display. When the snails are side on to one another they drive calcareous darts, often called 'love-darts', into the body wall of the other. This somehow stimulates them into mating.

Above: Many lower forms of life can increase their numbers by simply dividing into 2. This process is called asexual reproduction. The nucleus in *Amoeba* divides **(1)** with the daughter nucleii moving apart **(2)** as the rest of the cell separates and forms 2 daughter cells **(3)**. The young adult protozoans **(4)** can repeat the process in 3-4 days.

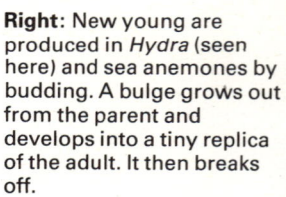

Right: New young are produced in *Hydra* (seen here) and sea anemones by budding. A bulge grows out from the parent and develops into a tiny replica of the adult. It then breaks off.

R **Ribbonworms** are some 750 species of the phylum Nemertina, related to the FLATWORM. Some are more than 20 metres long. Most species live in shallow waters.
Roundworms are some 10,000 species of worms with long bodies, pointed both ends and covered by a thick horny cuticle. They may be parasitic or free living, ranging in length from microscopic to over 1 metre.

S **Sea anemones** are related to the CORALS and do not have a free-swimming stage in their life cycle as do the JELLYFISH. They are amongst the most familiar of the COELENTERATES because they are easily seen in tidal rock pools.
Sea cucumbers are some 900 species of elongated, armless ECHINODERMS. Tube feet near the mouth are adapted as tentacles and trap small animals.
Snails and slugs are gastropods, part of the MOLLUSCA phylum. Snails have a single shell whereas slugs are shell-less. A typical snail shell is a conical shape with spiral markings.
Sponges of the group PORIFERA are classified into 3 types. The calcareous sponges have a support of chalk (calcium carbonate). They are either straight or with 3 or 4 branches. Glass sponges have their skeleton composed of hard bits of silica, each having 6 branches. These often fuse to give a lattice structure. The horny sponges have a jelly-like substance between the cells and a skeleton which is a combination of silica and a horny substance called spongin.

Squids are close relatives of CUTTLEFISH and OCTOPUSES. Like the former, they have 8 short and 2 long arms. The long arms wrap up prey after the powerful beak-like jaws have severed the nerve cord of a fish. They are able to change their colour and patterning to match surroundings. The giant squid of the North Atlantic is said to reach 20 metres in length.
Starfish and BRITTLE STARS are some 4,500 species of ECHINODERMS. Most have 5 arms radiating from the central disc, though some have as many as 40. They have remarkable powers of regeneration. Provided 20% of the central disc is attached to an arm, an entirely new adult starfish will slowly grow. Most species are carnivorous.

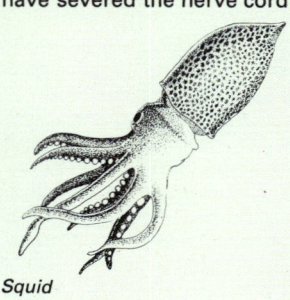

Squid

Ecology is the study of animals and plants in their natural habitats. By studying an animal as part of an animal and plant community, we can better understand the inter-relationships which hold together the delicate balance of nature.

Adaptation to Environment

Deserts: Fennec fox

Temperate forest: Red deer

Tropical forest: Toucan

Mountains: Mountain goat

Polar regions: Seal

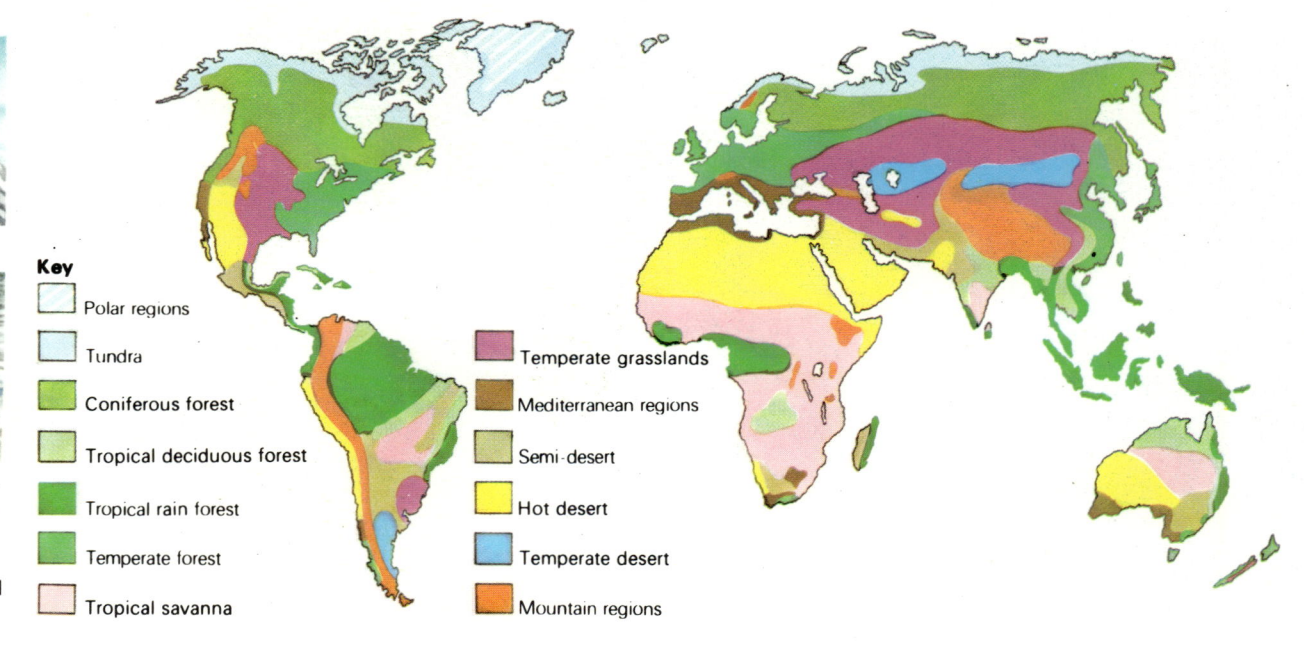

Right: The major biomes of the Earth are climatic zones each supporting its own specially adapted plants and animals.

Ecologists – scientists that study plants and animals in their natural habitat – have found that each region has its own kinds of plants and animals adapted to its particular climate and surroundings. These animal and plant communities are called "biomes" and the map shows the world's major biomes. Ecologists do not always agree on the exact number of biomes found in the world, some identifying a far greater number than shown here. However, it is generally accepted there are nine major land biomes: the polar regions, the TUNDRA, the CONIFEROUS FORESTS, the DECIDUOUS FORESTS, the TROPICAL FORESTS, TEMPERATE GRASSLANDS, TROPICAL GRASSLANDS, the deserts and the dry scrublands. The waters of the world are usually divided into the fresh waters, the seashores and the oceans.

The succession of vegetation from the equator to the two poles follows a certain pattern. At the equator we find tropical forest, next deciduous forest, then coniferous forest. Then we find grasslands and these areas merge polewards into the area of mosses and lichens, often called the tundra. The same pattern of succession in vegetation is found from the base of a tropical mountain to its peak as the climate changes with the increase in altitude.

Animal adaptation to its environment

The shape and size of an animal's body is usually adapted to its natural surroundings. A warm-blooded bird or mammal has to ensure that its body temperature remains constant. Adequate insulation in the form of fur, feathers or fat is therefore essential. The larger the animal, the more slowly it loses heat. So the Arctic POLAR BEAR is twice the weight and size (2.5 metres in length and half a tonne in weight) of the sun bear that lives in the tropical forests of south-east Asia. Also the polar animals have much thicker fur than their tropical relatives in order to

Key
- Polar regions
- Tundra
- Coniferous forest
- Tropical deciduous forest
- Tropical rain forest
- Temperate forest
- Tropical savanna
- Temperate grasslands
- Mediterranean regions
- Semi-desert
- Hot desert
- Temperate desert
- Mountain regions

Reference

A Adaptation is a characteristic that aids the ability of a plant or animal to cope with its environment.
Adaptive radiation is the evolutionary diversification into a variety of ecological roles of species which all have the same common ancestor. For example, the 12 species of finch on the Galapagos Islands evolved from a seed-eating ground finch from South America. Each species is adapted to a particular niche. One finch feeds on cactus, another on seeds, and one species uses a twig to poke out grubs.
Antarctica is the south polar region, the large frozen continent which sprawls over the 'bottom' of our planet. Apart from a few invertebrates, the only animals that have adapted to the Antarctic conditions are seals, penguins and some sea birds. These are all carnivores, feeding on the rich plankton and fish stocks of the Antarctic seas.
Arctic is the north polar region, the Arctic Ocean and its surrounding ring of land. The only non-migratory mammals to be found are polar bears, Arctic foxes and members of the seal family.

B Blind cave fishes have lost their power of full sight due to becoming adapted for a life in the total darkness of cave pools. They

School of dolphins

find their way about without bumping into anything by using their sensitive lateral line system (*see page 38*).

C Camels are adapted for DESERT life with broad, heavy feet that do not sink into sand, nostrils that can be closed to keep out flying sand, and interlocking eyelashes that protect the eyes against both Sun and sand. They can go for considerable distances without water, drawing on the fat reserve in their humps for an energy source.
Chromatophores are

50 Adaptation to Environment

Right: Plants and trees in a jungle are stratified, or layered, and different kinds of animals live in more or less restricted vertical ranges. Each layer has its own characteristics. Animals that live in south-east Asian forests are shown here.

insulate the body, keeping heat in and cold out.

Cold-blooded animals – the invertebrates, fishes, amphibians and reptiles – work more efficiently when warm, but must gain heat from their environment as they are unable to produce heat themselves. Few of these species are found in cold climates, the majority being adapted for warm and tropical biomes.

Tropical forests

Animals living in tropical rain forests, often called jungles, have many problems. Quick movement is rather difficult where these tall trees grow quite close together and are laden with hanging vines and lianas. As a result the animals living there, either blend in with their surroundings as they hide from enemies, or they are well adapted for moving through the branches of the trees. Monkeys, with their gripping hands and balancing or 'prehensile' tails, are very agile among the middle layers of the forest canopy. Certain apes, such as the small gibbons, chimpanzees and orang-utans, all have long arms for swinging from branch to branch. Sloths have adapted to hang upside down and in their South American home stay on one tree as long as it has enough foliage for them to eat. Their fur is encrusted with a green algae which acts as a camouflage among the leaves. Reptiles and amphibians abound, together with tree snakes, tree frogs and numerous lizards. This biome is a haven for birds, which tend to have vivid colours. At a distance, a brightly-coloured bird on a branch could be taken for a tropical flower and it is not until it flies that its identity is revealed. Insects are numerous in the jungle, each one adapted to a particular niche.

Temperate forests

Evergreen forests are made up of conifers such as spruces, firs, pines and hemlock. They are found to the south of the moss and lichen tundra across Eurasia, Alaska and Canada. Many animals of these regions are adapted to eating parts of the conifers. Birds such as redpolls and crossbills feed on the seeds of the cones. Woodpeckers

---

specialized cells in the skins of certain animals, such as flat fishes, reptiles, amphibians and octopuses, that contain various pigments. Each chromatophore is bounded by an elastic membrane and its size and shape is controlled by special muscles. When light intensity in the surroundings alters, a message is passed through the eye, via the nervous system to the chromatophores which expand (spreading more pigment) or contract (spreading less pigment) to blend the animal's skin to the new environment.

Climbing perch were so named because when the first ones were found in trees it was thought they climbed there unaided. Later it was realized that they had been dropped there by crows or kites. However, they do leave the water to move from pond to pond, using their strong gill covers like arms and pushing with their pectoral fins and tail. They have air-breathing chambers connected to their normal gills and must have atmospheric air to survive.

Colour change in animals is usually brought about by CHROMATOPHORES. Other changes occur as part of the process of becoming an adult. For example, a gull loses its brown juvenile plumage by moulting and growing new white feathers.

Other birds and mammals, such as PTARMIGANS and Arctic foxes, change their coats gradually to match the different seasons. These animals change from brown to white in autumn, thus making them well camouflaged for Arctic winters. Many birds grow bright coloured feathers for the courtship season, the more vivid decorations being usually worn by the males.

Coniferous forests are characterized by long, cold winters and short warm summers. The animals of this type of biome are often

Camels in the Libyan Desert

Adaptation to Environment 51

Left: The great diving beetle is adapted for an aquatic life, although it still breathes air. It pushes its abdominal tip just above the surface, raises its wing covers and draws air into a pair of breathing pores (spiracles). It also traps air under its wing covers as a reserve.

extract grubs and insects from the bark. Mammals such as squirrels also take the seeds as part of their diet. Insects abound in coniferous forests; often one species has adapted to feed on a particular species of conifer.

In deciduous forests there is a mixture of trees such as oak, birch, beech and ash. These trees shed their leaves in the autumn, and so there is more light available for animals living on the ground. More plants are able to grow on these forest floors than in the jungle and coniferous forests, so that a greater number of animals inhabit this area. These include well-known animals such as foxes, badgers, squirrels, deer, and ground-nesting birds such as pheasant and woodcock. The canopy layer is home for many birds such as woodpeckers, warblers, tits, owls and buzzards. Each bird species is adapted to its own type of feeding, so that there is little competition.

The polar biome

There is little vegetation within the polar regions. Without brief periods of warmth, only the simplest plants can grow. Most animals are therefore flesh-eaters, such as the polar bears and Arctic foxes of the northern lands, and the fish-eating penguins of the Antarctic. In the northern polar region most of the animals feed on the tundra during the short summer and then move south when the snows come again. The musk-oxen, snowy owls, ptarmigan and snow buntings are some of the few animals that can remain on the tundra all the year round.

The grassland biomes

In the areas where there are very few trees and stretches of open grassland, the animals must be able to move quickly as there is so little cover. There are large areas of grassland on all the continents. The tropical grasslands are called savannas, while in the cooler parts of the world they are termed prairies, plains or steppes.

The grasslands of temperate regions were formerly very large, but most areas in the Northern Hemisphere have been ploughed up for

Right: The woodpecker is so named because it chips holes in trees to prey on insects or to make a nesting hole. When a hole is drilled, the long flexible tongue then darts forwards and its tiny barbs and sticky saliva at the tip catch the prey. The tongue can extend 4 times the length of the bird's upper beak and runs back inside its head.

---

climbers or adapted for a life on the forest floor. Common climbers include tree squirrels. On the forest floor roam

Red squirrel

wolves, bobcats, and black and brown bears. Insects are abundant in summer and provide a food supply for the many bird species.

Convergent evolution occurs when similar animal characteristics are developed over long periods of time in species that live in the same kind of environment but in different areas of the world. For example, the toucans of the South American tropical forest look very similar to the hornbills of African and Asian tropical forests, although they are not closely related.

Termite mounds

Deciduous forests are made up of a mixed variety of trees that need warm summers, mild winters, and a moderate rainfall well spread out over the year. Insects abound in summer and include butterflies and moths and their caterpillars, bugs and beetles.

Deserts are very dry areas where days are very hot and nights are quite cold. As the Sun sets, the temperatures can fall from a sizzling 56°C to 0°C. Deserts cover almost 20% of the Earth's surface and are not as lifeless as many people suppose. The adaptation of animals in this biome is concerned mainly with getting enough water and to avoid burning up in the middle of the day. Special adaptations include longer legs to keep away from the burning sands or the ability to fly onto plants.

52 Adaptation to Environment

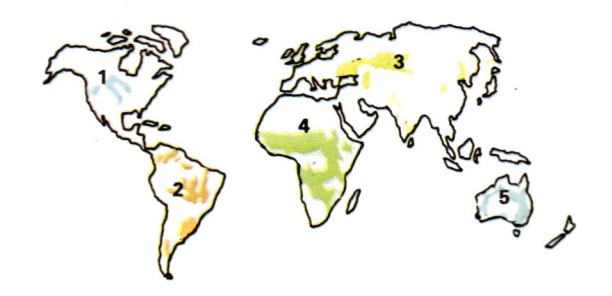

agriculture, grazed by cattle, or built on. In the Southern Hemisphere, domestic herds have become dominant over the natural animal life. It is very interesting that the same environment around the world has produced similar looking animals, although they are not closely related. This is because as the various animal species evolved in the grassland environment of the different continents, and as the conditions were predominantly the same in each, they ended up with the same adaptations and thus looked very similar. This is known as 'CONVERGENT EVOLUTION' and the chart on the right shows many examples.

Dry lands and deserts

Where the rainfall is too low to support the tropical grasslands, there is a gradual change through temperate grasslands to scrub, to semi-desert and then to dry arid deserts. The scrublands have their own unique animals. In Australia there are some curious marsupials (pouched mammals). The koala lives on a diet of eucalyptus leaves alone. The FENNEC FOX is adapted to living in the desert. Its huge ears help to keep it cool. Most desert animals have to avoid the heat by burrowing or hiding during the day. Many obtain moisture from desert plants, as water is very scarce. Thus, the majority of these animals are nocturnal, moving and feeding during the cooler night. Many cold-blooded reptiles bask in the Sun's heat in these areas in order to raise their body temperature to a level suitable for activity.

Strange relationships

Within each biome there are various small-scale habitats, such as the life in a tree, a fallen log or a rock pool. Within each habitat, certain animal species are adapted to a certain way of life. The place where an animal lives and its behaviour

1 North America — Prairie dog, Pocket gopher, Woodchuck
2 South America — Tuco tuco, Viscacha

Burrowing Mammals

When the fauna of grasslands on different continents are compared, it is noticeable that many different unrelated species living there look alike. They have evolved similar adaptions for life in similar environments although these are separated by oceans.

Rhea

Flightless Birds

Jack rabbit

Leaping Herbivores

American bison — Alpaca

Large Herbivores

Cougar, Coyote — Crab-eating fox, Bush dog

Large Carnivores

Predators drink blood from their prey, while herbivores 'drink' water from desert plants such as cacti.

F Fennec foxes are adapted for DESERT life. Their pale short coats and huge ears pick up the slightest sound in the hours of darkness when they hunt for food. The ears also help to cool them when their bodies get overheated.
Fresh water biome includes the temporary rainpools of desert regions, ponds and streams to an enormous inland mass of water, such as the Caspian Sea. The oxygen content varies from one part of a lake to another. This can be caused by the type of plant life, currents or lake-bottom material. In a rapid stream there is lots of oxygen in the bubbling, rushing waters but the animal must be able to cope with the strong currents.

G Grasslands cover nearly 50% of the land area in the Southern Hemisphere. There are also great areas of flat, open country in the Northern Hemisphere.

Jackal

Speed is the first important adaptation of large mammals such as antelopes, zebra and deer. This enables them to escape from enemies such as cheetahs, lions and packs of jackals, all good running carnivores. Many small mammals have adapted to jumping along instead of running, using long strong back legs and balancing tails. Even some birds have evolved into runners, from the flightless ostriches and emus to the long-tailed roadrunners of the south-west United States.

H Hermit crabs are more closely related to lobsters and shrimps than true crabs. The long tail has become adapted to hold the hermit to the inside of an empty shell. When disturbed, the hermit draws back into its shelter leaving only its pincer claws showing. They change shells at frequent intervals to keep up with their growth. They often provide a moveable home to certain species of sea anemone. This is not a chance association. The anemone gives the crab camouflage while the

Adaptation to Environment 53

3 Asia	4 Africa	5 Australia
Mole rat / Hamster	Golden mole	Marsupial mole / Wombat
	Ostrich	Cassowary
Asiatic jerboa	Springhaas	Grey kangaroo / Wallaby
Wild horse	Gnu	
Tiger	Lion	Tasmanian devil

anemone is transported to new feeding grounds.

Jacanas, or lily trotters, are tropical birds with very long toes and straight claws. These enable them to walk easily over floating vegetation without sinking.

Mimicry is where an animal resembles some other animal, plant or even object in its environment. It is used to deceive predators or prey and can confuse the creature with the object that it mimics. Stick insects, for example, look like the twigs on which they live. False coral snakes are not poisonous but their red, black and white bands down their bodies mimic the venomous coral snakes.

Nocturnal creatures are those animals that are active during the hours of darkness (from dusk to dawn). Nocturnal primates, such as the tarsier and loris, have huge eyes (necessary to achieve a high degree of stereoscopic vision) and excellent hearing so that they can detect both food and enemies, and find their way about the branches of their tree home.

Ocean biome is the term given to the huge marine zone. The animals and plants usually live and move in one of 4 different ways. Some float at the surface, travelling from place to place using the currents and surface winds. Others are adapted to swimming and include most fishes, seals, whales and penguins. Others crawl on the ocean floor, for example worms, starfish and molluscs. There are also the deep-sea dwellers which have adapted in bizarre ways to ensure survival. The female angler fish ensures that a mate is available for reproducing by having a dwarf parasite male angler fish attached to her body.

Okapis of the Congo TROPICAL FORESTS exhibit disruptive coloration. This breaks up the animal's body outline and makes this shy animal more difficult to see by a predator.

Oxpeckers are African starlings that feed exclusively on ticks that live on mammals such as antelopes, rhinos and hippos.

Pilot fishes are so named because of their peculiar habit of appearing

Hermit crab

54 Adaptation to Environment

there is called its niche. For example, the niche of an adult barnacle is being attached to a rock, feeding from the water current when the tide is in, and closing its shells when exposed to the air or to the flow of the outgoing tide.

In certain habitats animals have entered into some strange relationships. One well-known partnership is that of the colourful tropical anemone fishes and certain tropical sea anemones. These tiny fishes (some called clown fishes are illustrated *above*) live in and around the anemone's stinging tentacles, being curiously immune to its lethal barbs. The body of these fishes is believed to be covered with a mucus or slime secreted by certain glands of the fish, which inhibits the action of the stinging cells. In return for this protection, it tempts other fish into the anemone's tentacles.

Anyone who has been fortunate enough to visit an African game reserve will probably have seen egrets travelling upon the backs of cattle, elephants or antelopes. These birds catch the insects that are disturbed by these large herbivorous mammals. Although Africa is the original home of these cattle egrets, they have

Above: The remora is perfectly adapted for hitching rides on fishes. Its dorsal fin acts as a sucker and attaches the remora to its host's body.

Below: Red-billed oxpeckers feed on ticks off their Brahman cattle host and in return give warning calls when any danger threatens.

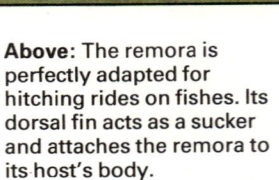

Above: Red clown fish swim fearlessly among the sea anemone's stinging tentacles. The fish are protected by a mucous covering which inhibits the action of the stinging cells.

to direct the course of sharks and other large fishes. It is unlikely that they really do this, but they do benefit from the food scraps of the shark's leftovers and to some extent are protected by them.

Polar bears are adapted for the extremes of Arctic life with thick white coats, hairy soles on their feet and small ears that do not lose too much heat to the outside.

Ptarmigan are small grouse of the Arctic tundra and brushlands. They are unique in having their toes and legs completely feathered, supposedly an adaptation for walking in soft snow. They live on berries, buds, seeds and lichens. They are typically grey-brown in summer and white in winter.

Red grouse and young

S Scrubland is a fringe biome between hot deserts and tropical grasslands, sometimes referred to as semi-desert. The rainfall is very irregular and when it does come, plant life bursts into bloom and lower animals such as insects reproduce rapidly under the improved conditions. There are large stretches of scrub in Australia, this mallee scrub providing a habitat for many birds such as bell birds and mallee fowls. These fowl incubate their eggs in a 'compost' of rotting vegetation.

Seashore is the biome where land meets the ocean and is the area between the high and low tide marks. The rich variety of animal life living between the tides is exposed to sharper contrasts of environment than any other living creatures. They must withstand wave action when the tide is in, and drying out by the wind and Sun when the tide is out.

Sloths are members of the Edentata order that are renowned for their slow movements. A sloth clearly in a hurry was timed at 4 metres a minute. The sloth is

Above: A camouflaged female praying mantis waits motionless pretending to be a twig, until an insect passes by. It then suddenly jack-knifes its front legs out to grasp the prey. Mating is a hazardous business for the male mantis as he is liable to end up being eaten as well.

been introduced by man into other countries of the world, such as America and Australia, where they have been seen following tractors to catch the disturbed insects.

Some of the most curiously shaped insects are the 1,800 species of praying mantis. The various species are perfectly coloured and often shaped to match their background. They can sit motionless, totally camouflaged, waiting for an innocent fly or other insect to come within reach. Then the folded front limbs shoot out to grasp the victim.

As in the mantis, it is often the way an animal feeds that has produced some strange adaptation. Chameleons are slow-movers but perfectly camouflaged in their African and Madagascan tree homes. Their limbs do not shoot out but the muscular tongue is the organ which shoots out and catches prey. Vampire bats have evolved to feed only on blood. They silently alight at night near a sleeping victim, such as a domestic cow or giant ant eater, and climb up gently to bite a piece of skin from a relatively hairless area such as the neck region. The victim's blood does not clot as the bat feeds due to an anti-coagulant in the bat's saliva.

Left: A chameleon changes its colour in response to light intensity and this often results in a better blend with its background.

---

adapted to a life of hanging upside down in trees. Its hair grows backwards from the belly towards the back to prevent the fur becoming waterlogged. Its coat has a greenish tinge from the algae that live in the fur and this aids camouflage.

Taiga is the term given to the vast stretches of evergreen forests that grow right across northern Europe, Asia and northern America, just south of the tundra.

Temperate grasslands was the term formerly used for the Great Plains or prairies of North America and the vast steppes of Eurasia. Today, most of these areas are farmland, although the untamed and untouched regions still support a unique range of wildlife. Before the settlers came, huge herds of bison

Swallow

Red fox

56 Adaptation to Environment

Blend and bluff camouflage

We have seen numerous examples of animals that are camouflaged to blend in with their surroundings and avoid predators. If they keep still, an observer finds it very difficult to detect them. There are thousands of insects looking like leaves, green grass, flowers or even sticks, these various disguises helping them to survive longer and reach their goal of producing young and ensuring the survival of their kind. Many ground-nesting birds are camouflaged so that they are hidden when on their nest and incubating the young.

Few mammals draw attention to themselves by being brightly coloured, and most of the young are very well camouflaged indeed. This is because most mammalian young are unable to run and feed when born, and must remain hidden until strong enough to accompany their parents. Young fawns are usually spotted when they are born in order to blend in with their patchy background. At this stage they give off no scent either, so that a hunting fox or bear will not be able to find them.

An animal's camouflage pattern is not always fixed. Some animals can change colour and blend with their background. This is mainly true of fishes and includes plaice and halibut and other flat fishes, as well as octopuses and some other molluscs. On land lizards, such as chameleons and anole lizards can change colour. The reason for this occurrence is due to changes in light intensity in the surroundings.

Warning colours

Some insects, snakes, fishes and frogs, and one or two lizards, are poisonous or distasteful to eat, and these are usually brightly coloured. This warns other animals that they are to be left alone. However, the predators have usually had to learn this fact by trial and error. For example, wasps, cinnabars and their caterpillars are bold yellow or red and black. It has been shown that predators quickly associate the bright colours with a bad taste and leave them alone. Another strange adaptation is where harmless insects and snakes have evolved similar colours to the poisonous ones. They gain protection from mimicking the poisonous species, but the extent of this protection is open to a good deal of argument.

Above: The bright colours of an arrowpoison frog from the jungles of South America warn predators of its deadly venom. The poison is used on Indian arrows and can paralyze animals as large as monkeys.

Below: The eyespots on a peacock butterfly provide it with effective protection. They may scare away enemies, such as small birds.

---

and pronghorn antelope roamed the prairies. A large rodent population is adapted to prairie and steppe life and includes prairie dogs, ground squirrels and gophers.

Tropical forests are the zones we often call jungles. The constantly warm temperatures and frequent rainfall are very important to the diversity of animal life. The giant trees tower over 60 metres high and animals are adapted to life in the various layers from the tree tops to the jungle floor. Rivers are plentiful in this environment and many animals, for example tapirs, peccaries and capybaras (both South American rodents) will take to water to avoid being caught by predators such as jaguars.

Tropical grasslands are often called savannas and large areas are found in Africa, as well as South America and Australia. These grasslands have dry seasons and the animals living here must be able to survive periods of drought. The African savanna is extremely rich in animal life, many of the mammalian species being quite large. These include elephants, zebra, gnu and buffalo as well as many kinds of antelopes and gazelles. There are also many predators such as lions, cheetahs and hyenas and jackals.

Tundra is the inhospitable biome that runs around the edges of the ice-covered Arctic. The lower layers of the tundra earth are permanently frozen and are called permafrost. There is a 4 month summer during which time plant life flourishes, insects abound and these support a large influx of birds such as waterfowl, finches, buntings, larks and warblers.

Indian elephant

Throughout history, many species have become extinct as better adapted species replaced them. But man has created a crisis in the natural world. Today, we are just beginning to understand the dangers of upsetting the balance of nature.

Man and Animals

Man, *Homo sapiens,* has existed on the Earth for only about 300,000 years. During this time he has used and been useful to many other animals. Certain parasites such as fleas and bugs may live on his body; others such as tapeworms and flukes can live inside his body. Some animals such as crocodiles, tigers and lions may kill him, while man has hunted birds, mammals and fish for thousands of years for food and clothing.

An interesting aspect of man's involvement with animals, is the fact that he has been able to tame several species to work for him. The domestication of animals has been going on for over 10,000 years and probably wolves and jackals were the first animals to be domesticated. In the Stone Age, man was still a nomadic hunter and the wolf existed over a wide area throughout Europe and Asia, down to peninsular India, and in North America. Man and the wolf, therefore, often came into contact. The earliest domestication of dogs probably took place in south-west Asia and when man reached Australasia in the Middle Stone Age he took some with him. Some escaped and returned to a wild state and these are the DINGOS we know today. Wolves and dogs probably first associated with man to feed off the remains from the kills of early tribesmen. Possibly men reared puppies they found, at first keeping them as sources of food when times were hard. No doubt men realized their worth as watch dogs and later used them to seek out prey. They were also trained to herd and protect other domestic animals such as goats and sheep. By the time the dog reached Europe, about 6000 BC, it was probably already performing the duties of a sheepdog.

Today there are over 165 BREEDS of dog which have been bred for racing, coursing, carrying, guiding, herding, retrieving, guarding as well as just for being a faithful friend for man. There is

Above: Dogs are popularly called man's best friend.

Above: Horse-riding is a popular sport throughout the world.

Above: South Americans use llamas on rocky terrain.

Above: Indian elephants are trained to work in forests.

Above: Camels are widely used in dry climates.

Above: The Lapps depend on reindeer for their livelihood.

Reference

A Aye ayes are cat-sized and do not look like primates at all, although their nearest relatives are the lemur-like indris. They are nocturnal creatures, living in the tropical forests of Madagascar. They have claw-like nails on the 5 digits of each foot. They have rodents' incisors to bite holes into the bark and the extra-long middle digit of the hands extracts any grub. Probably less than 50 exist.

B Blue whales are the largest of all mammals but despite being totally protected probably less than 2,000 survive. They were the most avidly hunted whales between 1920-40 as they were the biggest and gave the greatest quantity of oil. In 1930 it was estimated between 30-40,000 existed.
Breed is a race or strain of a domesticated animal which continues to breed true only if crossed with breeds having the same hereditary qualities.

D Dingos are the wild dogs of Australasia, about the size of a collie, standing about 50 cm at the shoulder. They vary in colour from light red to brown and yellow-brown. Although rewards were given for killing them as they killed sheep and cattle, they are still common.

Dodos were flightless turkey-sized birds that lived on the island of Mauritius. Sailors hunted the dodo for food, and pigs destroyed its eggs. It had become extinct by 1681.

E European bison, also known as the wisent, were almost exterminated in the truly wild state. They once ranged over western and southern Europe, east to the Caucasus and north to Siberia. They were saved just in time by being protected in the 1930s. Today, numbers are healthy, the majority of them living in the

Java sparrow

Dingo

now a breed available to suit almost anyone, wherever he lives and whatever he does.

In domesticating wild animals, man has always selected certain characteristics that he would like to be reduced or accentuated in future stock. For example, from the point of view of domestication, one problem is the fierceness and aggressive nature of most wild animals. This has been reduced to a minimum by selective breeding. The inborn traits of certain domesticated animals such as the CAMELS, reindeer and yaks have not been greatly altered because their value to man is that they are particularly well adapted to their environments. The reindeer has not had its instinct to migrate bred out of its system. Instead, the Laplanders have adapted to the reindeer's life and lead a nomadic life following the semi-domesticated reindeer herds on their journeys. The working elephant of the Asian timber forests has also not been changed, but each new offspring is taught the logging trade during its first 15 years of life, its adolescent period of growth.

Most domesticated animals, however, have been bred to provide meat, milk or skins, or to be draught animals or beasts of burden. The many breeds of pig are all descended from the fierce forest-dwelling wild boar. Today they are strikingly different from their wild ancestors. They are less hairy, shorter-legged, fatter and have quite differently shaped heads. They fatten more easily and reproduce at a greater rate than their wild cousins.

All domestic horse breeds probably originate from the species *Equus caballus*. PRZEWALSKI'S HORSE is the only surviving representative in the wild of the original species. It exists in small numbers on the Mongolian steppes, as well as in captivity. Donkeys, mules and asses have been man's beasts of burden for centuries. They are still used to carry people and goods in poorer countries, but in most developed countries, donkeys are sometimes kept as pets for children.

Sheep, goats and cattle belong to the same family as buffaloes and antelopes. It is not known which wild sheep is the ancestor of modern breeds but the mouflon probably provided the main breeding stock centuries ago. Sheep are valued commercially for their mutton and wool, and in some countries for their milk. Goats are valued either for their fleece or their milk, the cashmere and the angora breeds being the most important goats, reared for their soft, fine wool.

Domestic cattle are known to have existed in Babylon as early as 5000 BC. In continental Europe, domestic cattle were bred from the wild aurochs, enormous long-horned beasts that stood 1.8 metres at the shoulder. The last known wild specimen was killed in Poland in 1628. A very ancient breed which survives in a few places is the 'wild' white cattle which was probably brought into Europe by the Romans, although some zoologists think it is a direct descendant of the wild auroch. However, today the numerous breeds of domesticated cattle are kept for their milk, meat and hides, and also as beasts of burden in poorer countries.

Some animals are very difficult to breed in captivity and are usually caught when young and then tamed. These include those animals we usually refer to as exotic pets. The ancient Egyptians, for example, kept falcons, cheetahs and mongooses. FALCONRY is a popular sport in many countries today, but has led to the poaching of young protected birds-of-prey from their nests in many countries, so seriously endangering various species such as the peregrine.

Endangered species

Over the last few hundred years many hundreds of species of plants and animals have disappeared from the Earth. Some have become EXTINCT naturally during the course of evolution. However, man has been responsible for much of

Left: The sport of taking a quarry using a bird-of-prey was practised in the East as long ago as 1200 BC. It became the sport of kings and aristocracy in the West during the Middle Ages. A peregrine falcon is seen here ready to take off.

Right: All dogs belong to the same species and wild wolves were probably their original ancestor. Working dogs such as those illustrated are most important to man, but many 'toy' dogs have been bred purely as pets. The earliest domesticated dogs probably resembled the Australian dingo. These are descended from the dogs that Stone Age man took to that continent from Asia about 8,000 years ago.

Right: Domestic pigs originate from the wild boar of Eurasia and south-east Asia. The earliest known domesticated pigs existed in Neolithic times. Selective breeding brought about a less hairy skin and the loss of tusks. Pigs are valued almost solely as meat producers, but the meat is used in different ways. Bacon pigs are longer bodied, rather higher on the legs and a lighter colour than a pork animal of similar age.

Right: The origins of sheep are not known for certain. The view most widely held is that the Asiatic mouflon provided the foundation stock, but the Urial and Argali are sometimes regarded as its ancestors. Domestic sheep are valued for their mutton and wool, and occasionally also for their milk. With some breeds, such as the Merino, wool is the primary product, while other such as the Southdown are kept mainly for their mutton, and wool is a secondary consideration.

Bialowieza Forest in Poland and various zoos. A woodland animal, it browses on ferns, leaves and bark.
Extinct animals are those that have died out completely. This can happen naturally due to changes in the environment to which an animal cannot adapt. Man's pressure on wildlife has altered the rate of extinction so that now many more species are endangered. Animals are hunted for food, sport, pharmaceutical use, or because they are considered vermin or pests. Others have been killed by various types of pollution and the destruction of their habitat.

Black rhinoceros

F Falconry is the hunting sport that uses falcons, such as the peregrine, in open country. In former times it was a sport of gentlemen and kings. It still is widespread in the Middle East. Today poachers take fledglings to train as the bird is very difficult to breed in captivity. Pesticides and other toxic chemicals have also taken their toll on the population. Although protected and no longer in danger of extinction, the peregrine's chances of increasing in number are still uncertain.

G Game reserves or game parks have been established in most countries of the world to protect the wildlife living in that region.
Giant pandas were first introduced to the western

Leopard

Man and Animals 59

Right: The cattalo, half cow and half bison, was bred in the USA in the late 1880s. It did not prove to have the beefier qualities of its longhorn mother and the sturdy and hardy characters of a bison. Sadly, the offspring were stillborn or sterile and those that survived were very bad tempered. The idea soon floundered.

Bison

Longhorn

Cattalo

The **wolf** is probably the ancestor to early breeds such as terriers.

The **husky** was originally bred in Greenland for sledge pulling.

The **alsatian** is widely used as a guard dog and for police work.

The **rough collie** is used for sheep work.

The **red setter** is used as a gun dog for retrieving.

The **wild boar** was the fierce forest ancestor to modern pigs.

The **Berkshire** breed originated in the Thames Valley, England, for meat.

The **Landrace** was selectively bred for bacon by the Danes.

The **middle white sow** was bred from Yorkshire breeds.

The **Tamworth** is bred in the Midlands for high quality bacon.

The **Asiatic mouflon** was probably the original ancestor of the modern-day sheep.

Jacob's sheep was an early breed that is quite rare today.

The **Southdown** is a short-wool breed with excellent meat.

The **Leicester** is the oldest long-wool breed, dating back to the 1700s.

The **Merino ram** is a long-wool breed that is very popular in Australia.

---

world by Père David, the French missionary, in 1869 when he returned from China. These pandas look like bears but they are actually related to the racoons. Their range is restricted to the bamboo forests in an isolated mountainous region of western Szechwan in China. Little is known of their breeding habits in the wild but the Chinese have bred several in captivity and probably the future of this attractive mammal is ensured. Over 20 specimens are in captivity, the majority being in China.

Golden lion marmosets are the most brightly coloured of all living mammals – an intense, shimmering golden yellow. They are found in the coastal forests of south-eastern Brazil where numbers are below 400. Their decline is due to deforestation and the capture of live specimens for the animal trade. Although protected in Brazil it may be too late to save this primate.

Green turtles are marine reptiles of warm seas that come ashore to tropical sandy beaches only to lay their large clutches of eggs. It is impossible to estimate current numbers but there has been a severe drop over the last 25 years. Their decline is due to demand for the adult's cartilage for soup, their oil for cosmetics and skin for leather. Eggs are taken in thousands from beach nests and the young that hatch are preyed on by birds, fish and crabs. They are now protected in some nesting and feeding areas, such as in Queensland, Australia, where 5,000 km of beach and 2,000 km of the Great Barrier Reef are designated refuges.

IUCN, or the International Union for the Conservation of Nature is the major conservation body now trying to preserve nature in the wild, and natural resources all over the world. It was started in Brussels in

White-bearded gnu and young

Man and Animals

Aye aye — *Golden lion tamorin* — *Mountain gorilla* — *Asiatic lion* — *Tiger*

this destruction because he has altered their environment or killed them in such numbers that they have not been able to survive. Today, one in every 40 species of birds and mammals is in danger of dying out. Many other animal groups such as amphibians, reptiles and fishes also have many species in danger of becoming extinct due to man's pressures.

Man hunted wild animals originally for food and clothing, and later just for sport or to be put in museums or zoos. Other animals have been destroyed because they have been looked upon as vermin, or poisoned by PESTICIDES designed to exterminate weeds or insect pests. The disappearance of many species has been caused by man's destruction of habitats, by felling trees for timber, or by increasing the agricultural or urban land area, or digging up land for building purposes.

Today, two major international conservation bodies are trying to preserve nature in the wild as well as our dwindling natural resources. These are the International Union for the Conservation of Nature and Natural Resources (known as the IUCN) and the WORLD WILDLIFE FUND (WWF). Through their work in raising funds and helping to convince countries to pass and enforce conservation laws, many animals are now protected from being harmed or endangered by man.

The orang-utan, a large ape with a reddish coat, is one of the most endangered species of mammals in south-east Asia (the islands of Sumatra and Borneo). Its numbers have dwindled in the wild mainly due to its tropical rain forests being destroyed to increase agricultural land and because poachers now kill adult females to obtain the live young for the animal trade. However, the numbers now being bred in captivity are encouraging and plans to return zoo-bred specimens to the wild are underway, although it is very difficult to encourage tame specimens to become independent of man.

The TIGER of China, northern Asia and India is in a serious plight at the moment due to trophy-hunters, and habitat destruction. Although less than 2,000 survive in India, they are now protected. The largest of all tigers, the nomadic Siberian tiger, hunted for the pharmaceutical trade, used to range from Siberia through Mongolia to Korea and Manchuria. Its population is now stable in only one protected mountain system in Korea, a remote corner of Manchuria and some protected areas of the far eastern USSR.

Everything in nature is interdependent. It is impossible to destroy anything – to fell a tree or bulldoze a patch of wasteland, without affecting innumerable creatures and upsetting nature's delicate balance. For example, because of man's interference in killing natural predators, certain

Above: The main causes for the threatened survival of these endangered species are trophy-hunting, forest destruction, the capture of live specimens for the animal trade, killing outright for man's needs or being directly in competition with man and his domesticated animals.

Below: The European bison, or wisent, almost became extinct due to the hostilities of the First World War. From a protected nucleus its numbers were rebuilt to a fairly healthy level. It survives mainly in zoos and the Bialowieza Forest in Poland.

1934. One of its major tasks has been to collect information about species in danger of extinction and begin action to prevent total loss. The IUCN co-operate with the WORLD WILDLIFE FUND and governments to conserve endangered species. For example, the POLAR BEAR is now protected by the countries in which it ranges – the USA, Canada, Norway and the Soviet Union.

Japanese crested ibises are some of the rarest birds in the world. They are confined to Sado Island and possibly the Noto Peninsula, Japan. Once they were found across northern China, Manchuria, Korea and Japan. They declined to 8 known specimens this century with the deforestation of their favoured wooded wetlands and virgin forests. They are unlikely to survive in the wild.

Mauritius kestrels are small falcons that have declined to drastically low numbers as they were shot for supposedly killing chickens. The species may well be extinct.

Mountain gorillas are the largest and most powerful of all living primates and inhabit the dense remote forests of West Africa. Their decline is due to shooting by local tribesmen for food, by animal traders wanting the young, and also through forests being taken over by agriculturalists. Females only bear young every 3 to 4 years so the reproduction rate is not very high.

National Parks are areas of protected land, found worldwide. The first to be established was the Kruger National Park in South Africa, an area the size of Wales or Belgium, and now still among the finest and most visited national parks.

Nature reserves are areas set up mainly in European

Female mountain gorilla

Man and Animals 61

Javan rhino
Blue whale 
Green turtle 
Mauritius kestrel
Japanese crested ibis

Below: Due to better political relationships with China, where the giant panda survives in the wild, more pairs of this delightful animal are being displayed in western zoos, having been donated as gifts to visiting dignitaries. Peking Zoo has had great success breeding them in captivity, but the first baby born in the west only occurred in 1977 at Chicago Zoo in the USA.

animals such as rabbits and rats, have increased abnormally in number and do millions of pounds worth of damage to crops every year. The introduction of new animals can also destroy the habitat itself, as in the Galapagos Islands where the voracious goat has destroyed areas of trees and bushes which support other wildlife.

In many areas of the world man has spoilt the basic natural resources such as water, air or soil by polluting them to such a degree that the balance of nature has been upset. For example in

Above: The flightless dodo, once common in Mauritius, became extinct in about 1680. It was hunted by sailors for sport and food, and its nesting sites were disturbed by pigs.

Below: Przewalski's horse is the sole survivor of the wild horse. Species exist in many major zoos throughout the world and they may be re-introduced into the wild later this century.

Banff National Park, Canada

countries to protect the wildlife that lives within its area. They range from the size of a small pond to millions of hectares in area.
Né-Né, or Hawaiian goose, was saved from extinction by breeding the 30 survivors in captivity and then later reintroducing some into their native islands. It is now the official bird of the state of Hawaii.

○ **Oil pollution** is still a serious threat to marine animals. Birds suffer the most, because as well as being totally clogged with oil so that they are unable to move and feed, their feathers may be damaged so they are no longer waterproof. This causes the bird to become waterlogged and drown.
Orang-utans are heavily-built primates with a reddish coat that live in the jungles

Né-Né

Arabian oryx

Man and Animals

many cities, such as Tokyo and San Francisco, the pollution by smoke from homes, factories and car exhaust fumes, was so great that the health of people was seriously affected. Some governments have now passed Clean Air Acts so that air pollution is becoming less of a problem, although enforcement is not always easy.

Oceans and freshwater rivers and lakes are still endangered, however, due mainly to factory and home waste and OIL POLLUTION. Oil leakages from tankers or sea oil rigs are a common event these days and the damage to marine life is enormous. The *Amoco Cadiz* in 1978 spilt 250,000 tonnes of oil into the sea off Brittany. The beaches were polluted and chemical dispersants were used to break up the oil. Although every effort is made to 'mop-up' such a disaster, thousands of seabirds and fish perish. The

Above: One way in which the survival of a species can be ensured is by studying its habits in the wild. Here a black rhinoceros female and young are being filmed in the Serengeti.

Above left: The Trans-Amazonian highway crosses about 2,000 km of virgin tropical rain forest in almost a straight line from Belem in northern Brazil to Brazilia. The opening up of these new areas to man's exploitation must endanger the survival of more animal species.

problems created by polluted fresh water range from outbreaks of disease in animals to the destruction of the habitat and the disappearance of fish and other wildlife in the area. Facing the dangers of contamination, the United States, Great Britain and West Germany have taken the lead in constructing long-range programmes to try to avoid future catastrophies and counteract present polluted areas.

Whales, the mighty monarchs of the oceans, have not disappeared due to the polluted sea but due to overhunting by man. Some species have been reduced to such low numbers that although now protected, they may not survive as they cannot reproduce quickly enough to ensure that their numbers increase. The 20th century has produced the greatest slaughter of whales. It was intensified at the beginning of the century to such

---

of Sumatra and Borneo. People cannot now keep them as pets; they are sent to centres where they are retrained for life in the wild.

Oryx is the name given to 3 species of rare gazelles. The Arabian oryx is the smallest and rarest, its decline being mainly due to the discovery and extraction of oil from its habitat. The other 2 are the scimitar-horned and the beisa oryx (more common).

Ospreys, or fish hawks, are examples of protected birds of prey. They were formerly killed because it was thought that they took domestic animals. Now, 24-hour watches are kept on nests in the breeding season.

Wolf

P Passenger pigeons thrived in their millions in their native North America until the late 19th century when they were shot and ruthlessly slaughtered. The last died in captivity in 1914.

Pesticides poison many land animals who may eat them unknowingly. Often the chemical DDT is absorbed and builds up in the animal's body.

Pollution is usually brought about as a by-product of man's activities. The air is polluted by smoke such as sulphur dioxide and waste gases. Water is damaged by

Polar bears

Man and Animals 63

Below: The culling of seals is an emotive subject at the moment. A certain amount of culling may be beneficial in lowering the infant mortality rate in rookeries due to overcrowding. However, the cubs are clubbed to death to avoid damaging the seal skin. Many people believe this method is cruel and should be stopped.

Right: Although many whales such as the blue, right, humpback and grey are totally protected, their numbers are so very low that they might not be large enough to ensure their survival. Closed hunting seasons and size of catch limits protect the other species to some extent, but numbers still fall.

Right whale 10,000 / 2,000
Blue whale 210,000 / 13,000
Fin whale 450,000 / 100,000
Sperm whale 1,000,000 / 620,000
Humpback whale 100,000 / 7,000
Grey whale 15,000 / 11,000

1946   1976

an extent that the North Atlantic right whale (*Eubalaena glacialis*) was virtually exterminated. A hundred years ago, a whaler's three-year trip netted him 37 whales. Today, with modern detecting equipment, weapons and fast boats, a whale a day (even three or four) is the usual catch. At the present time, whaling is theoretically a regulated industry with each country being allowed a catch of a specified number of whales a year. In principle, all species are protected by international agreements arrived at by the International Whaling Commission. However, the USSR and Japan are not conforming to the agreed terms, despite pressures from conservation bodies and governments of other nations.

GAME RESERVES, NATURE RESERVES and NATIONAL PARKS are found all over the world today so that animals and plants can exist within a protected area in their natural habitat. There are, of course, still problems from poachers and from thoughtless people who may start fires, or disturb breeding animals by going too close.

Throughout the world, man has put at risk areas from a few square metres to thousands of millions of hectares. In Britain millions of kilometres of hedgerows have been destroyed to create large-scale fields so that modern agricultural machinery can function. In the Amazon basin in South America the forest is being cut down and long roads penetrate the dense jungle which was hitherto considered to be unassailable. Here the whole forest life is at risk. However, some local, national and international organizations are beginning to see that this work must be curbed before the balance of nature is destroyed forever.

Above: Oil pollution caused by disasters, such as the running aground of the Amoco Cadiz off northern France in 1978, causes the death of millions of birds, as well as marine creatures.

poisoning by industrial effluents, or by deoxygenation due to the decomposition of organic matter such as sewage.
Polar bears are dwellers of the Arctic tundra and ice-bound north pole region. Their numbers became severely reduced due to game hunting. Recently they were being shot from helicopters. Then their habitat was interferred with by the opening up of the northern polar region for oil. Polar bears are now protected by the countries in which they are found and numbers are increasing.

Przewalski's horse is the only wild horse to survive in the wild, mainly in Outer Mongolia. Numbers in captivity now ensure its survival. Its decline in numbers was due to hunting for meat and being bred with domestic ponies.

Q Quaggas were a common zebra species which used to graze the grasslands of the veldt of South Africa. When colonizers moved in, this mammal with its striped neck and head was killed indiscriminately because it competed with the cattle for food. The last specimen died in captivity in 1883.

S Siamese crocodiles survive only on a crocodile farm in Thailand. Most crocodile species are endangered because their skins make excellent leather.
Spanish Imperial eagles are distinguished from other large eagles by their white shoulders. Not known to breed outside Spain (where total numbers are less than 100), they are protected only in Coto Doñana National Park. Seven pairs have nested there in the cork oaks. The species will not survive without protection.

Booted eagle

T Tasmanian wolves, or thylacines lived in captivity until the 1930s although none were bred. Their decline was due to settlers shooting them as they preyed on sheep flocks. Although occasional sightings have been recorded in the western part of Tasmania, they are probably extinct.
Tigers are depleted in number over most of India, northern Asia and China. Probably less than 2,000 survive today. The decline is due to trophy-hunting, poaching for the fine skin,

Man and Animals

Below: Oil pollution from supertankers that have collided or broken up at sea are almost weekly happenings around the world. The crude oil sticks to the birds' feathers and bills thus preventing them from flying and fishing.

Below: Rivers all over the world have become polluted to such a degree that most of the aquatic life including fishes, plants and insects are endangered. The main cause of the pollution is the release of highly toxic industrial wastes and town sewage.

Below: Rubbish heaps have thousands of tonnes of waste poured on them every day. Much of it is leftover food and this attracts rats as well as flies and birds. Fleas living on rats transmit diseases such as the plague and typhus.

Below: Open-cast mining, deforestation and agricultural programmes have destroyed the natural habitat of many wild animals, causing their numbers to be reduced often to the point of endangering the species.

Below: Air pollution threatens not only birds and insects but also man. Some of the intermediate chemicals in the complex process of producing plastics and similar oil derivatives are frighteningly toxic if released into the air.

destruction of the natural habitat and because of their supposedly man-eating and cattle-killing habits. They are now legally protected over most of their range, and some reserves have been established. However, they will quite probably be extinct in the wild by the year 2000.

Trumpeter swans are the largest North American swans. At one time numbers were down to below 60 in the states excluding Alaska, but now total over 2,000. Hunting was the major cause of decline. Un-

Gila monster, a poisonous lizard

doubtedly this bird was saved by the creation of the Red Rock Lake refuge in Yellowstone Park, Wyoming, USA, in 1935.

Whooping cranes are rare North American birds that breed on remote sub-Arctic lakes and migrate 3,700 km to winter in Texas.

Unfortunately they risk being shot by sportsmen on the way in mistake for sandhill cranes.

World Wildlife Fund, or WWF, was started in the 1960s when it became obvious that something had to be done to halt the growing threat of extinction facing large numbers of plants and animals, and also to reduce the rate at which natural habitats were being destroyed by man. Its main task is to raise money to finance conservation action. The headquarters are in Switzerland with branches worldwide.

World Wildlife Fund emblem

Index

66 Index

Page numbers in **bold** type refer to the reference sections. Page numbers in *italics* refer to illustrations.

A
Aardvark, **9**, *9*, 10
Acorn worm, *45*
Adaptation
  Animals, 49–56, **49**
Adaptive radiation, 4, **49**
Adder, **26**, *26*, *28*
Agama lizard, **26**, 29, 31
Agnatha, 33
Albatross, **17**, 18, *19*, *22*, 25
Alligator, 26, 29
Alpaca, *52*
Alpine
  Chough, *7*
Alsatian, *59*
American
  Bison, *52*
Ammonites, *4*
Amoeba, *3*, **45**, 46, 48, *48*
Amphibians, **26**
  Age of, 4, *5*
  Anurans, 26, 30
  Axolotl, **26**, *27*, 32
  Behaviour, 32
  Breathing, 26
  Caecilians, 26, **27**
  Endangered, 60
  Environment, 50
  Evolution of, *5*, 26
  Feeding, 27
  Frogs, **28**
  Groups, 26
  Habitat, 26
  Newts, 26–7, 30, **30**, *30*
  Poisonous, 32
  Reproduction, 26, 29–30
  Salamander, 26–7, 30, **31**
  Toads, 26–7, 29, **31**, *31*
  Urodelans, 26
Anaconda, *6*, 7
Angel fish, **33**, *33*
Angler fish, **33**, *37*
Anhinga, **17**
Animals
  Adaptation, 49–56
  Amphibians, 26–32
  Kingdom, 3, **3**, *3*
  Arthropods, 39–44
  Birds, 17–25
  Chordata, 3, **3**
  Endangered, 58–64
  Environment, 3, 4, **4**, 49–56
  Evolution, 4, **5**, *5*
  Extinction, 4, **5**, **58**
  Fastest, 8, *8*
  Fish, 33–8
  Insects, 39–44
  Invertebrates, 45–8
  Mammals, 9–16
  Man and, 57–64
  Record holders, 6–8
  Reptiles, 26–32
  Size of, 6–7
  Species, 3, *3*, **8**
  Speed of, 7–8, *8*
  Vertebrates, 3, **8**
Annelids, 45, **45**, *45*, 47
Anole lizard, **26**, 56
Ant, **39**, 42, 44
Ant lion, **39**
Antarctica, **49**
Anteater, **9**, *9*, *12*
Antelope, 9, **9**
  Gerenuk, 12
  Migration, 16
  Speed of, 8
Anurans, 26, 30
Apes, **9**, 10, 50
Aphid, **39**, *39*
Arabian oryx, *61*
Arachnida, *39*, **39**
  See also Spiders
Archer fish, **33**, 35, *35*
Arctic, **49**
Aristotle, **3**
Armadillo, **9**, 10
Arrowpoison frog, **26**, *56*
Arthropods, 39–44, **39**
  Arachnida, **39**, *39*
  Characteristics, 39
  Chilopoda, *39*, **40**
  Classes, *39*
  Collembola, *39*
  Crustaceans, *39*, **41**
  Diplura, *39*
  Diplopoda, *39*, **41**
  Eyes, 44, *44*
  Feeding, 41
  Flight, 39–41
  Group behaviour, 41–2
  Hearing, 44
  Heaviest, 7
  Insects, *39*, **42**
  Life cycles, 42–3
  Merostomata, *39*, **42**
  Metamorphosis, 43, *43*
  Migration, 42, *43*
  Movement, 39–41
  Onychophora, *39*
  Pauropoda, *39*, **43**
  Protura, *39*, **43**
  Senses, 44, *44*
  Species, 39, *39*
  Symphyla, *39*
  Thysanura, *39*
Artiodactyla, **9**, *9*
Aschelminthes, **45**, *45*
Asiatic jerboa, *52*
Avocet, **17**, *17*
Axolotl, **26**, *27*, 32
Aye aye, **57**, *60*

B
Baboon, **9**, *9*, 10, *11*, 14, 15
Barber fish, 36, *36*
Barnacles, 8, **39**, 54
Barracuda, **33**
Basilisk, *27*
Bats, *9*, **10**
  Flight, 9–10, 12
  Hearing, 13, *13*
  Hibernation, 16
  Migration, 16
  Vampire, 55
Bear, *9*, **10**, *10*
  Adaptation, 49
  Feeding, 13
  Movement, 10
Bearded lizard, **26**
Beaver, *9*, 10, **10**, *10*
Bee, 39, **39**, 42, 44
Beech, 51
Bee-eater, **17**, 24
Beetle, **39**, *42*, *51*
Biome, 49, *49*
Birch, 51
Bird of paradise, **17**, *17*, 23
Bird of prey, **17**
Birds, 17–25
  Anatomy, 17–8, *17*
  Beaks, 20–1, *20*
  Behaviour, 22–3
  Breeding, 24–5
  Camouflage, 23, 56
  Communication, 23
  Courtship, 23, *23*
  Eggs, 17, 24–5, *25*
  Endangered, 60
  Evolution of, *5*
  Fastest, 8, *8*
  Feeding, 20–1, *20*, 51
  Feet, *20*, 21
  Flight, 17–9, *18–9*
  Largest, 6, *6*
  Migration, 15, 22–3, *22*
  Nests, 24, *24*
  Reproduction, 24–5
  Singing, 23
  Smallest, 6, *6*
  Species, *3*, 9, 17
  Tropical forest, *50*
Bison, **10**, **57**, *59–60*
Bivalves, **45**, 46
Blackbird, **17**, 21, 24, *25*
Black rhinoceros, *58*, *62*
Blind
  Cave fish, 38, **49**
  Snakes, **26**
Blue whale, 6, *6*, **57**, *61*, *63*
Boa constrictor, **27**, 28
Boar, 58, *59*
Bobolink, **17**, *22*
Booted eagle, *63*
Bowerbird, **17**, 24
Brachiopoda, *45*
Brain coral, *45*, 47
Breed, 57, **57**
Bristletail, *39*, **40**
Bristleworm, **45**, 47
Brittle star, 45, **45**
Brotulid, *7*
Bugs, **40**, 41, 57
Bullfrog, **27**
Bush dog, *52*
Butterfly, **40**, *40*, *50*
  Fish, **33**, *33*
  Life-cycle, 43, *43*
  Migration, 42, *43*
  Proboscis, 41, *41*
  Tortoiseshell, *7*
Buzzard, **18**

C
Caecilians, 26, **27**
Caiman, 26–7, **27**
Cambrian period, **3**
Camel, **10**, **49**, *50*, *57*, 58
Camouflage, 56
Carboniferous period, **3**
Caribou, **10**, 16
Carnivores, **10**, 12–3
  Arthropods, 41
  Fish, 34
Carp, **33**, 38
Cassowary, 18, **18**, 21, *21*, *53*
Cat, 10, **10**, *13*
Catfish, 33, **33**, *33*, 36–8
Caterpillar, 42–3, *43*
Cattle, 10, **10**, 58, *58*
Cetaceans, *9*, **10**, 13
Chaffinch, 22
Chameleon, 27, **27**, *27*, 29, 31, *31*, 55, *55*, 56
Cheetah, **8**, *8*
Chelonia, 26–7, **27**
Chicken, **18**, 20
Chilopoda, *39*, **40**
Chimaera, **34**, *34*
Chimpanzee, 10, **11**, *11*, 13, 50
Chiroptera, *9*, **11**
Chondrichthyes, 33
Chordata, 3, **3**
Chromatophore, **49**
Cicada, *40*
Cichlid, **34**, *37*
Classification, **3**, 4
Cleaner fish, 36, *36*
Climbing perch, **50**
Clown fish, 54, *54*
Cobra, 28, **28**, 29
Cockatoo, **18**, *18*
Cockroach, **40**, *40*, 41, 43
Cod, 34, **34**, *36*, 37
Coelacanth, *6*, **34**
Coelenterates, 45, **45**, *45*, 46, 48
Collembola, *39*
Collie, *59*
Colour
  Change, **50**, 56
  Warning, 56
Colugo, *see* Flying lemur
Condor, **18**
Conifer, 50
Coniferous forest, 49, *49*, **50**, 51
Convergent evolution, **51**, 52, *52–3*
Coral, *3*, 8, **46**, 47
Cormorant, 18, **18**, *18*
Cougar, *52*
Courtship
  Amphibians, *30*
  Arthropods, 42–3
  Birds, 23, *23*
  Fish, 37, *37*
  Mammals, 14
  Reptiles, 29
Coyote, *52*
Crab, *3*, 7, *39*, 40, **40**, 41
Crab-eating fox, *52*
Crayfish, **41**
Cretaceous period, **3**
Crocodile, 6, 26, 28, **28**, 29
  Siamese, **63**
Crossbill, **18**, *18*, 20, 50
Crow, **18**
Crustaceans, *39*, **41**, 44
Cuckoo, **19**, *22*, 23
Curlew, **19**
Cuttlefish, 46, **46**, *46*
Cuvier, Georges, **3**

D
Daddy-long-legs, **41**
Damselfish, 36
Darwin, Charles, 4, **4**, 47
Deciduous
  Forest, 49, *49*, 51, **51**
Deer, 9, **11**, 12–4, *49*
Dermoptera, *9*, **11**
Desert
  Animals, **49**, *49–50*, **51**, 52
Devonian period, **4**, 26
Dinosaurs, 4, **4**, *5*
Dingo, 57, **57**, *57*
Diplopoda, *39*, **41**
Diplura, *39*
Dodo, **57**, *61*
Dog, **11**, *15*
  Breeds of, 57, *59*
  Movement, 10, *11*
Dogfish, **34**
Dolphins, *9*, 10, **11**, *13*, *49*
Ducks, 21, 25
Dugong, **11**

E
Eagle, 18, **19**, *19*, 21 *63*
Earthworm, *45*, **46**, 47, 48
Echidna, **11**
Echinoderms, *3*, 45, *45*, 46, **46**
Echolocation, 13, *13*
Ecology, 49
Edentata, *9*, **11**
Edible frog, **28**, *32*
Eel, **34**, *34*, 36
Eggs
  Amphibian, 29, *30*
  Arthropods, 42–3
  Birds, 24–5, *25*
  Earthworm, 48
  Fish 37
  Mammals, *see* Monotremes
  Reptile, 29, *29*
Electric eel, **35**
Elephant, *9*, **11**, *15*
  African, *12*
  Family grouping, 15
  Food consumption, 12
  Indian, *56–7*
  Migration, 16
  Size of, 6, *6*
  Speed of, *8*
Embryology, **4**
Emu, 18, **19**
Endangered species
  Animals, 56–64
Environment, **4**
  Animals, 3–4, 49–56
European bison, **57**, *60*
Evolution, **5**
  Amphibians, 26
  Classification of species, **3**, 4
  Convergent, **51**, 52, *52–3*
  Darwin, Charles, 4, **4**
  Dinosaurs, 4, **4**
  Feathers, 17
  Fish, 33
  Lamarck, Jean, 4, **6**
  Living fossils, 4, *4*, **6**
  Marsupial, 4
  Natural selection, 4, **7**
  Reptiles, 26
  Theories of, 4
  Uniformitarianism, 4, **8**
  Wallace, Alfred, 4, **8**
Extinction, 4, **5**, **58**
Eye
  Compound (Insect), 44, *44*
  Fish, 38
  Human, *46*
  Mammals, 13
  Octopus, *46*
  Scallop, *46*
  Snake, *28*, 31

F
Falconry, **19**, 58, **58**, *58*
Feathers, 17
Feeding
  Amphibians, 27
  Arthropods, 41
  Birds, 20–1, 51
  Echinoderms, 46
  Fish, 34–6
  Insects, 41
  Mammals, 12–13, 51
  Molluscs, 46, *47*
  Reptiles, 27–8
Fennec fox, *49*, 52, **52**
Fiddler crab, **41**, 42, *43*
Finch, **19**, 20
Fishes, 33–8
  Age, 33
  Behaviour, 36–8
  Breathing, 35–6, *35*
  Classes, 33, *33*
  Courtship, 37, *37*
  Eggs, 37
  Environment, **53**
  Evolution, *5*, 33
  Eyes, 38
  Fastest, 8, *8*, 34
  Feeding, 34–6
  Fins, 33–4
  Flat, 35, *35*
  Flying fish, *8*, **35**
  Gills, 35, *35*, 36
  Hearing, 38, *38*
  Migration, 36, *36*
  Movement, 33–4, *34*
  Poisonous, **38**, *38*
  Reproduction, 36–8, *37*
  Sailfish, 8, *8*
  Senses, 38
  Species, *3*, 9
  Speed, 8, *8*, 34
  Teeth, 34, *34*, 35
Flagellate, *45*
Flamingo, **19**, *20*, 21
Flatfish, **35**, *35*
Flatworm, 45, **46**
Flea, 41, **41**
Flies, 41, **41**
Flight
  Birds, 18–9, *18–9*
  Insects, 39–41
  Mammals, 9
Flycatcher, **19**
Flying
  Fish, *8*, 34, **35**
  Lemurs, 12, **12**
  Lizard, *50*
  Squirrel, 12, *50*
Forest
  Coniferous, 49, *49*, **50**, 51
  Deciduous, 49, *49*, 51, **51**
  Temperate, 50–1
  Tropical, *49–50*, 50, **56**
Fossils, **5**
  Living, 4, *4*, **6**
  Palaeontology and, 4, **7**
Fox, **12**, *14*, *55*
  Habitat, 51–2
Fresh water biome, **52**
Frigate bird, 18, **19**, 23, *23*
Frilled lizard, **28**, *31*
Frog, 26, **28**
  Amphibian, as, 26
  Arrowpoison, **26**
  Bullfrog, **27**
  Edible, **28**
  Habitat, 50, *50*
  Movement, 27, *32*
  Painted reed, *32*
  Poisonous, 32
  Reproduction, 29, *30*
  Tadpoles, *30*
Frogmouth, **19**, *20*, 21

G
Game reserves, **58**, 63
Gaur, *50*
Gecko, **28**, *28*
Geese, **20**, 22, *22*
Gerbil, **12**
Gerenuk, 12
Gestation periods, *15*
Gharial, 26, **28**, *28*
Giant
  Hornbill, *50*
  Panda, **58**, *61*
  Tortoise, 29, **29**, *29*
Gibbon, 10, **12**, 50, *50*
Gila monster, **29**, *64*
Gills, 35, *35*, 36
Giraffe, 6, *6*, 12, **12**, 13
Gnu, **16**, *53*, *59*
Goat, **12**, 58
Golden lion
  Marmoset, **59**
  Tamorin, *60*
Golden mole, *53*
Goldfish, **35**, *36*
Goliath beetle, 7
Gorilla, *5*, 10, **12**, *15*, *60*
Grasshopper, *39*, 40–1, **41**, *41*
Grassland, 51–2, **52**, 71
  Temperate, 49, *49*, **55**
  Tropical, 49, *49*, **56**
Great auk, *5*
Great diving beetle, *51*
Greater crested newt, 29
Grebe, **20**, 23, *24*, 25
Green turtle, **29**, *29*, **59**, *61*
Greenfly, 41, **41**
Grouse, **20**, *20*, 25, *54*
Gulls, **20**

H
Habitat, **5**, 52, 61
  See also Environment
Hagfish, 33, **36**
Hammerhead shark, 38
Hamster, **12**, 16, *52*
Hare, *9*
Harvestman spider, **41**
Hawk, **20**
Hawk moth, *43*
Hearing
  Arthropods, 44
  Birds, 21, *21*
  Fish, 38, *38*
  Insects, 44
  Mammals, 13
Hedgehog, *13*, 16
Hemichordates, 45, *45*, **46**
Hemlock
  Conifer, 50
Herbivores, 12, *12*
Hercules beetle, *42*
Hermit crab, **52**, *53*
Heron, **20**, *20*, 21, 23
Herring, 33, **36**, 37
Hibernation
  Mammals, 16, *16*
  Reptilian, 31
Hippopotamus *9*, 13, **13**
Hooke, Robert, 4
Hornbill, 24, *50*
Horned viper, **29**
Horse
  Man and, *57*, 58
  Movement, *11*
  Przewalski's, *61*, **63**
  Wild, *53*
Horseshoe crab, **41**
Hummingbird, 19, *19*, **20**, 23
  Size, 6, *6*, 18
Husky, *59*
Hutton, James, 4
Hydroids, **46**, 48, *48*
Hyracoidea, *9*
Hyrax, *9*

I
Ibex, *12*
Ibis, 19, *61*
Iguana, 29, **29**, *29*, 31
Insectivores, *9*, 12, **13**
Insects, *39*, **42**
  Eye, 44, *44*
  Feeding, 41
  Flight, 39–41
  Group behaviour, 41–2
  Hearing, 44
  Heaviest, 7
  Life cycles, 42–3
  Migration, 42, *43*
  Movement, 39–41
  Pollination by, 102–3, *103*
  Proboscis, 41, *41*
  Senses, 44
  See also Arthropods
Invertebrates, **6**, 45–8
  Annelids, 45, **45**, *45*, 47
  Aschelminthes, **45**, *45*
  Brachiopoda, *45*
  Classes of, 45, *45*
  Coelenterates, 45, **45**, *45*, 46, 48
  Echinoderms, 45, *45*, 46–7, **46**
  Evolution, *5*
  Hemichordates, 45, *45*, **46**
  Molluscs, 45, *45*, 46, **47**, *47*
  Movement, 45–6
  Platyhelminthes, *45*, **47**
  Porifera, *45*, **47**
  Protozoa, 45, *45*, 46, **47**, 48
  Reproduction, 48, *48*
  Senses, 45–6
  Tunicates, 45, *45*
  See also Arthropods
IUCN, **59**, 60

J
Jacana, *53*
Jackal, **13**, 15, *52*, 57
Jack rabbit, *52*
Jacob's sheep, *59*
Jaguar, **13**

Index

Japanese crested ibis, **60**, *61*
Java sparrow, *57*
Javan rhino, *61*
Jellyfish, 45–6, **46**, *47*
Jungle, *see* Tropical forest
Jurassic period, **6**

K
Kangaroo, *3*, **13**, *15*, *53*
Kestrel, 19, **20**, *61*
Kingfisher, **21**, *21*, 23–4, *24*
Kiwi, *20*, **21**, 22
Koala, *9*, **13**, 14, **14**, *52*
Komodo dragon, *28*
Kori bustard, 6, 18
Krill, 6, *41*

L
Lacewing, 39, *40*
Ladybird, **42**, *42*
Lagomorpha, *9*, 13
Lamarck, Jean, 4, **6**
Lamp shell, *45*
Lamprey, 33, *33*, **36**
Lantern fish, **36**
Leaf-curling spider, *44*
Leech, 47, *47*
Lemmings, 10, **13**
Lemurs, 9, **14**
 Flying, 12, *12*
Leopard, **14**, *14*, *50*, *58*
Life, evolution of, 4, *5*
Linnaeus, Carolus, 4
Lion, *12*, **14**, 14, *53*, *60*
Lister, Martin, 4
Living fossil, 4, *4*, 6
Lizard, *30*
 Agama, **26**, 29, 31
 Anole, **26**
 Basilisk, *27*
 Bearded, **26**
 Behaviour, 31
 Chameleon, **27**, *27*, 29, 31, *31*, 55, *55*
 Frilled lizard, **28**, *31*
 Gecko, **28**, *28*
 Iguana, **29**, *29*, **29**, 31
 Komodo dragon, *26*
 Protective colouring, 56
 Skink, **31**
Llama, **14**, *57*
Lobster, 39, *39*, 40, **42**
Locust, 41–2, **42**, *43*
Loris, *50*
Lungfish, 36, **36**, *36*

M
Macaw, *20*, **21**
Malayan moon rat, *50*
Mallard, *20*
Mallee fowl, **21**
Mammals, 9–16
 Camouflage, 56
 Carnivores, 12–3
 Cetaceans, *9*, 10
 Characteristics of, 9
 Endangered, 58–64
 Evolution of, *5*
 Feeding, 12
 Gestation periods, *15*
 Hearing of, 13, *13*
 Heaviest, 6, *6*
 Hibernation, 16, *16*
 Insectivores, 9, *12*, **13**
 Marsupials, 9, *9*, **14**
 Migration, 15–16
 Monotremes, 9, *9*, **14**
 Orders of, *9*
 Primates, *9*, 10, **15**
 Reproduction, 14–5
 Rodents, *9*, **15**
 Senses of, 13
 Social life, 15–6
 Tallest, 6, *6*
 Ungulate, 10
 Vision, binocular, 13, *13*
Man
 Animals and, 57–64
 Intelligence, 3
 Walking, 10
Man-eating shark, **36**, **38**
Manatee, *9*
Marsupials, 9, *9*, **14**
 Evolution of, 4
 Gestation period, 14, *15*
 Habitat, *52*
 Mole, *53*
 Mauritius kestrel, **60**, *61*
 Megapode, 24
 Mendel, Gregor, **7**
Merino ram, *59*
Merostomata, *39*, **42**
Mesozoic era, **7**
Metamorphosis, 43, *43*
Migration
 Arthropods, 42, *43*
 Birds, 22–3, *22*
 Fish, 36
 Insects, 42, *43*
 Mammals, 15–6
Mildew, 85–6
Millipede, *39*–40, **42**
Mimicry, **53**
Mite, **42**
Mole, *9*, 10, *10*, **14**, *53*
Mole rat, *53*

Molluscs, 45, *45*, **47**
 Ammonites, *4*
 Movement, 46, *47*
 Senses, 46
Mongolian gazelle, 8, *8*
Monitor lizard, 29, **31**
Monkeys, 9–10, **14**, *15*, 50
Monotremes, 9, *9*, 14, **14**
Mosquito, 41, **43**, *43*
Moth, **43**
 Feeding, 41
 Hawk, *43*
 Migration, 42
 Smell, sense of, 44, *44*
Mountain gorilla, **60**, *60*
Mouthbrooder, **36**, *37*, *37*

N
Natural parks, **60**, 63
Natural selection, 4, *7*
Nature reserves, **60**, 63
Nectar, 41
Né Né, **61**, *61*
Nests,
 Birds, 24, *24*, 54
 Fishes, *37*
 Reptiles, amphibians and, *29*
Newts, 30
 Greater crested, **29**, *30*
 Reproduction, 30, *30*
Nightingale, **21**, *21*
Nightjar, 19, *21*, **22**
Nocturnal creatures, **53**

O
Ocean biome, **53**
Octopus, 46, *46*, **47**, *47*
Oil pollution, **61**, 62, *63*-4
Okapi, *53*
Onychophora, *39*
Opossum, 14, *14*
Orang-utan, 10, **14**, **61**
 Danger to, 60
 Habitat, 50
Ordovician period, *7*
Oropendola, *24*
Oryx, *61*, **62**
Osprey, **22**, *62*
Ostrich, *8*, 21, **22**, *53*
 Egg, *25*
 Flightlessness, 17, 18
 Size of, 6, *6*
Otter, 10, *10*
Owl, *18*, **22**
 Eyesight, 21
 Nest, 24
Oxpecker, **53**, *54*
Oystercatcher, 21, **22**

P
Palaeontology, 4, **7**
Panda, 13, **15**, **58**, *61*
Pangolin, *9*, **15**, *50*
Parakeet, **22**
Parasites, 3, *7*
Parrot, 21, *24*
Passenger pigeon, **62**
Passeriformes, 21, **22**
Pauropoda, *39*, *43*
Peacock butterfly, *56*
Peafowl, **22**, *23*
Pelican, **22**, *22*
Penguin, **22**, *25*
 Breeding, 24–5, *25*
 Flightlessness, 17
 Habitat, 51
Perch, climbing, **50**
Peripatus, *43*
Perissodactyla, *9*, **15**
Pesticides, 60, *62*
Pholidota, *9*, **15**
Pig, 58, *58*–9
Pike, 34, *37*
Pilot fish, **53**
Pinnipedia, *9*, **15**
Piranha, 34, **35**, *37*, 38
Pit viper, 28, **30**, *30*
Plaice, 35, *37*, 56
Plants
 Forest, *49*, **50**–1, *56*
 Species, **8**
Platyhelminthes, *45*, *47*
Platypus, *9*, 15
Plover, 21, *22*, *25*
Pocket gopher, *52*
Poison,
 Amphibians, 32
 Fish, **38**, *38*
 Pesticides, 60, **62**
 Snakes, *28*
 Spiders, 41
Polar bear, **54**, *62*, *63*
 Habitat, 3, 49
Polar region, 49, 51
Pollution, 62, **62**, *64*
Polyp, 46, **47**
Porcupine, *11*, **15**
Porifera, *45*, *47*
Portuguese man-o'-war, *45*, 46, *47*
Prairie dog, *52*
Praying mantis, 55, *55*
Pre-Cambrian period, *7*
Primates, 9, **15**
Proboscidea, *9*, **15**
Proboscis, 41, *41*
Protozoa, *45*, *47*

Movement, 46
 Reproduction, 48
Protura, *39*, **43**
Przewalski's horse, 58, *61*, **63**
Ptarmigan, 51, **54**
Pterosaurs, 4, **7**, *7*
Pufferfish, **37**, *37*
Puffin, **23**
Python, 28, 29, **30**

Q
Quagga, **63**
Quaternary period, *8*

R
Rabbit, 10, *15*, *52*
Racoon, **15**, *15*
Rattlesnake, 29, **30**, *30*, 31
Ray, 33, 34, *34*, 37, *37*
Red fox, *14*, *55*
Red setter, *59*
Red squirrel, *51*
Reindeer, *15*, 16, *57*, 58
Remora, **37**, *54*
Reproduction,
 Amphibians, 29–30
 Arthropods, 42–3
 Birds, 24–5
 Fish, 36–8, *37*
 Insects, 42–3
 Invertebrates, 48, *48*
 Mammals, 14–5
 Reptiles, 29
Reptiles, 26–32
 Agama, **26**, 29, 31
 Age of, 4, *5*
 Alligator, 26, 29
 Anaconda, 6, 7
 Behaviour, 31
 Caiman, 26, 27, **27**
 Chameleon, **27**, *27*, *27*, 29, 31, *31*, 55, *55*
 Chelonia, 26–7, *27*
 Courtship, 29
 Crocodile, 6, 26, 28, **28**, 29
 Eggs, 29
 Endangered, 60
 Environment, 31, 50, 52
 Evolution of, *5*, 26
 Feeding, 27–8
 Gharial, 26, **28**, *28*
 Iguana, 29, **29**, *29*, 31
 Largest, 6
 Lizard, *27*, **30**, 31, **31**, *31*
 Reproduction, 29
 Rhynchocephalia, *27*
 Snakes, **31**
 Terrapin, 26, **31**
 Tortoise, 26, **31**, **32**
 Tuatara, 4, *27*, **32**
 Turtle, 26, 29, **29**, *29*, **32**
Respiration
 Fish, 35–6
Rheas, **23**, *52*
Rhinoceros, 12, *12*, **15**, *58*, *62*
Rhynchocephalia, 27
Ribbonworm, **48**
Robin, 21, **23**, **23**, *23*
Rodents, *9*, 10, *12*, **15**
Roundworm, *45*, **48**

S
Salamander, 26–7, 30, **31**
Salmon, 33, *33*, **36**, *36*, **37**
Scallop, 46, **46**, *47*
Scorpion, *39*, 41, *43*
Scorpion fish, **38**, *38*
Scrubland, 49, 52, 54
Sea anemone, 46–8, **48**, *54*
Sea cucumber, *45*, **48**
Seahorse, 33–4, *37*, *37*, **38**
Seal, *9*, **16**
 Culling, *63*
 Depth of habitat, *7*
Seashore, *54*
Sea snake, 28, **31**
Sea slug, *47*
Sea spider, **44**
Sea squirt, *45*
Sea urchin, 45–7
Secretary bird, **23**
Senses
 Arthropods, 44
 Birds, 21–2, *21*
 Fish, 38
 Insects, 44
 Invertebrates, 45–6
 Mammals, 12–3
 Molluscs, 46
Shark, *33*, **38**
 Feeding, 35
 Movement, *34*
 Smell, sense of, 38
Sheep, 58, *58*–9
Shellfish, 8
Shrews, 12, *50*
Shrike, *22*, **23**, *23*
Shrimp, *7*, **44**
Sight
 Birds, 21, *21*
 Fish, 38
 Insects, 44
 Mammals, 13, *13*
 Molluscs, 46
 Octopus, 46, *46*
Silurian period, *8*

Silverfish, *39*, *39*
Sirenia, *9*, **16**
Skink, **31**
Skunk, 13
Sloth, **16**, 50, **54**
Slow loris, *50*
Slug, 46
 Sea, *47*
Smell, sense of,
 Arthropods, 44, *44*
 Birds, 21–2
 Fish, 38
 Insects, 44
 Mammals, 13
 Molluscs, 46
Snails, 45, *45*, **48**
 Mating, *48*
 Senses, 46
Snake, 28, **31**
 Adder, **26**, *26*
 Blind, **26**
 Boa constrictor, **27**, 28
 Boomslang, **27**
 Cobra, 28, **28**, 29
 Constrictors, 28, **28**
 Feeding, 27–8, *27*
 Hibernation, 31
 Horned viper, **29**
 Jacobson's organ, 28, *28*
 Largest, 6, *7*
 Moulting, *28*, 31
 Movement, 27–8, *27*
 Pit viper, 28, **30**
 Python, 28, 29, **30**
 Rattlesnake, 29, **30**, *30*, 31
 Sea snake, 28, **31**
 Sidewinding, *27*, 28
 Viper, 28, 29, **32**, *32*
Snipe, 23
Social behaviour
 Amphibians, 32
 Arthropods, 41–2
 Birds, 22–3
 Fish, 36–8
 Insects, 41–2
 Mammals, 15–6
 Reptiles, 31
Spanish imperial eagle, **63**
Sparrow, 20, **23**
Species,
 Animals, 3, *3*, **8**
 Arthropods, *39*
 Classification of, **3**, 4
 Endangered, 58–64
 Fish, 3, 9
 Invertebrate, *45*
 Mammals, *9*, 17
 Plants, **8**
Sperm whale, *7*, *63*
Spider, 41, **44**
 Crab, **44**
 Evolution of, *5*
 Feeding, 41
 Leaf-curling, *44*
 Movement, 39
Sponge, *3*, 45, *45*, **48**
Springhaas, *53*
Springtail, *39*
Squid, 46, **47**, *47*
Squirrel, *51*
 Flying, 12, *50*
 Habitat, 51
 Hibernation, 16
Starfish, 45, *45*, 46, **48**, *48*
Starling, **23**
Stickleback, 37, *37*, **38**
Stonefish, **38**, *38*
Stork, 18, 22, *22*, **23**
Streamlining, **8**
Sturgeon, 33, **38**, *38*
Swallow, *22*, 23, 24, **24**, *24*
Swallowtail butterfly, *40*, *50*
Swan, **24**, *24*
Swift, **24**
 Migration, *22*
 Speed of, *8*, *8*
Symphyla, *39*

T
Tadpole, *30*
Taiga, **55**
Tailor bird, 24, **24**
Tapir, *9*, 12, **16**
Tasmanian
 Devil, *53*
 Wolf, **63**
Temperate
 Forest, 50–1
 Grassland, 49, *49*, **55**
Termites, 42, *42*, **44**
Tern, **22**, 23, **24**
Terrapin, 26, **31**
Tertiary period, *8*
Thorax, 40, **44**
Thrush, 18, **23**, **24**
Thysanura, *39*
Ticks, *41*, **44**
Tiger, **16**, *63*
 Carnivore, *53*
 Danger to, 60, *60*
 Habitat, *50*
 Territorial marking, *13*
Tinamou, *24*
Toad, 26, **31**
 Altitude, maximum, *7*
 Feeding, 27

Movement, 27
 Reproduction, 29, *31*
Tortoise, 26, 31, **32**
 Giant, **29**, *29*, *29*
Toucan, *20*, **24**
Tree
 Frog, **32**, 50, *50*
 Shrew, *50*
Triassic period, **8**
Tropical
 Forest, 49, *49*, 50, *56*
 Grassland, 49, *49*, *56*
Trout, 35, **38**
Trumpeter swan, **64**
Tuatara, **4**, 27, **32**
Tubulidentata, *9*, **16**
Tuco tuco, *52*
Tundra, **56**
 Animals, 51
 Biome, 49, *49*
Tunicates, *45*, *45*
Turtle, 26, 29, **32**
 Green, **29**, *29*, *59*, *61*
Tyrannosaurus Rex, *5*

U
Uniformitarianism, 4, **8**
Ungulates, 10
Urodelans, 26

V
Vertebrates, 3, **8**
Viper, 28, 29, **32**, *32*
 Horned, **29**
Viscacha, *52*
Vision
 Binocular, 13, *13*
 Birds, 21, *21*
 Fish, 38
 Molluscs, 46
 Octopus, 46, *46*
 Insects, 44, *44*
Vulture, 18, *19*, **25**, *25*

W
Wagtail, 23
Wallaby, *3*, **16**, *53*
Wallace, Alfred, **4**, **8**
Warbler, **22**, **25**, 51
Wasp, 41, 42, **44**, 56
Water
 Beetle, 40, *51*
Weaver bird, 24, **25**
Whale
 Blue, 6, *6*, *57*, *61*, *63*
 Endangered, 62–3, *63*
 Food, 6, 16
 Killer, 13
 Migration, 16
 Sperm, *7*, *63*
White admiral butterfly, **40**
White-bearded gnu, *59*
Whooping crane, **64**
Wild boar, 58, *59*
Wildebeeste, *see* Gnu
Wings, 18, 19, *40*
Wolf, **16**, *57*, *59*, *62*
Wombat, *53*
Wood lice, **44**
Woodchuck, *52*
Woodcock, *21*, 51
Woodpecker, **25**
 Feeding, 50–1, *51*
 Habitat, 51
 Nesting, 24, *51*
World Wildlife Fund, 60, **64**, *64*
Worm, *3*, *39*, 45, *45*
 See also Annelids
Wren, **25**

Y
Yak, *7*, 58
Yellowhammer, **25**

Z
Zebra, 13, **16**, *16*

Acknowledgements

Contributing artists
Terry Callcut, John Goslar, Tim Hayward, Ron Haywood,
Kate Lloyd-Jones, Elaine Keenan, Abdul Aziz Khan

The Publishers also wish to thank the following:
A–Z Botanical Collection 4B, 18B, 33BL BR, 35B, 38L, 40BL BR, 34L, 36B, 41L, 43BL, BR, 44BR, 46, 58R, 60BL, 64BL
Heather Angel 9TR, 13, 16BL, BR, 19TR, 29BL, 31, 36, 39TL, 40, 42R, 43, 44BR, 50, 55T, 56L
Aquila Photographics 14B, 22B
Ardea 51C
Weisser 4T, Clem Haagner 19CL, I. Beames 39TR, Dr. Pat Morris 61T
Biophoto Associates 3, 9C, 10, 11T, 12, 23CR, 27, 44TL TR, 45TL TR, 55T
Anne Bolt 57B, 62L R, 63BL, 64BR
Bruce Coleman Ltd. 57T, Jen and Des Bartlett 26, S. C. Bisserot 30, Jane Burton 55C, Gerald Cubitt 33T, Oxford Scientific Films 19CR, Hans Reinhard 64TL
Robert Estall 17
Fisons 21
Brian Hawkes 6TL, 7R, 64C
Mark Lambert 47C, 63C
Natural History Photographic Agency 16TR, 25T, 48T C, 53C
Natural Science Photos 22T, 23CL, 25C, 45TR, 54L, 60T, 63T
Popperfoto 56B
Radio Times Hulton Picture Library 6BL
G. R. Roberts 7L, 32, 33L, 35T, 49T, 51T BR, 56TR
Harry Smith Horticultural Photographic Collection 14T
Spectrum Colour Library 6R, 23TR
Peter Stiles 53T
Thames Water Authority 18T
John Topham Picture Library 8LR, 9B, 11B, 15, 23BL BR, 24, 25BL BR, 28, 29BR, 31B, 34R, 37LR, 38R, 39BL, 41R, 42C B, 44BL, 45B, 47B, 48B, 49B, 50B, 51BL, 52, 53BL BR, 54B, 55B, 58L, 59, 60BR, 61BL BR, 63BR